The I-Ching
or
Book of Changes

Divined by Brian Burkea

For further information on the content of this book please contact:

Brian.burkea@gmail.com

What is IICMOV (International I-Ching Movement)?

IICMOV is an organization founded by the I-Ching itself and Brian Brukea. It is intended to provide guidance to those members of society that are interested in attaining Transcendence. Transcendence is by definition something above all caste and creed. It is the ultimate goal of all religions and the ultimate intention of the human form of life. There are many paths to Transcendence, and all paths require guidance; that guidance is available from of the I-Ching. Only one who has attained Transcendence can help those who have not; a scholar cannot help. Transcendence is very rarely attained, due to so much misguidance.

How to consult the I-Ching

Ideally the I-Ching should be consulted for the purpose of spiritual advancement, although it can also help us in other aspects of our lives. We should put aside our doubt of the unknown when consulting. The more we experiment with the I-Ching, the more the results will increase our faith in it. The more we put our faith in the I-Ching the more it can help us to improve our lives. We should be patient when consulting for we are conditioned to be sceptical of the unseen. Our faith in the I-Ching will naturally grow if we use it regularly and in time we will reap the fruit of that faith. Everything in our life will become auspicious the more we surrender ourselves to Divine Will. We all have a higher purpose; there is more to life than eating, sleeping, mating and defending. Materialism will never satisfy the eternal Self, for it is alien to our true nature. Only Transcendence can fulfil us.

The I-Ching may appear to be merely a book. But it is in fact offering a means to communicate with an ancient enlightened Sage. The Sage can give advice that is directly applicable to our life and our problems right now. The Sage can help us to learn the easy way rather than the hard way. The Sage can be our friend who truly has our best interests at heart. Transcendence is in our best interest and the Sage holds the key to that reality. The Sage holds the key to eternal bliss. Sage can help us to transcend our karma. We are all destined to be punished in the future for our misdeeds in the past, but by surrendering to Divine Will we can be forgiven. This world is a dangerous place and we are all in need of an infallible person to lead us out of it. By taking shelter of the Sage we will always feel safe and protected.

In order to use the I-Ching first you require 3 coins, a piece of paper and a pen.

1. Shake the three coins in your hands and drop them in such a way that they don't fly all over the place.
2. Decide which side of the coins you consider positive and which side you consider negative.
3. Count positives as three and negatives as two and add the value of all three coins.
4. If the number is odd, draw an unbroken line ———. If it is even draw a broken line — — .
5. Throw the coins again to get the second line and draw this line above, not below, the first line.
6. If the number is a six put a cross in your broken line — x — . If the number is a nine put a dot in your unbroken line —●—.
7. Repeat this procedure until you have six lines to form a hexagram.
8. Divide the six lines into a top and bottom trigram, ignoring the dots and crosses.
9. In the back of the book is a table which is a key for identifying your hexagram. The columns are the top trigrams and the rows are the bottom trigrams.
10. Find the column and row that relates to your trigrams.
11. Trace the column down and row across to the square where they meet. The number in this square ranges from 1 to 64, this is not a page number. In this book there are 64 messages which relate to the 64 possible hexagrams.
12. Find the message with the number that is given in the square.
13. Read the message and contemplate its meaning. If you asked for advice on a specific topic then meditate on how the message relates to your topic. If you asked for general advice then meditate on how the advice relates to your current mental state.
14. In your hexagram note which lines had a dot or a cross. Convert the dotted line to a broken line and the crossed line into a solid line.
15. Look up the message that is related to your new hexagram. This message further illuminates the first message.

TRIGRAMS

UPPER ▶ / LOWER ▼	CHEN — Heaven	KHEN — Storm	K'AN — Liquid	KAN — Solid	KUN — Soil	SUN — Wind	LI — Fire	TUE — Lake
CHEN — Heaven	1	34	5	26	11	9	14	43
KHEN — Storm	25	51	3	27	24	42	21	17
K'AN — Liquid	6	40	29	4	7	59	64	47
KAN — Solid	33	62	39	52	15	53	56	31
KUN — Soil	12	16	8	23	2	20	35	45
SUN — Wind	44	32	48	18	46	57	50	28
LI — Fire	13	55	63	22	36	37	30	49
TUE — Lake	10	54	60	41	19	61	38	58

CHIEN

HEXAGRAM 1

HEAVEN

HEAVEN

MEANING

The Supreme Person / God / Krishna / Siva / Brahma / The Higher Power

ADVICE

The Supreme Person is pleased with you. You are making good progress on the path to Transcendence. Continue to purify your consciousness. Remain patient in your practice, and tolerant towards others. Continue to endeavour to become more humble than a blade of grass. The mind may try to trick you at this point, remain very focused in your Practice.

IMAGERY

Heaven

ESSENCE

Heaven awaits you. Create a heaven on earth. Conquer your mind. Transcendence is possible. True happiness will soon be attained. Everything is Divine energy. You are an instrument of Divine Will.

PREDICTION

Human society will run out of oil in 2045

FIRST LINE   Don't relax your efforts. Happiness can be intoxicating. Maintain your equanimity. The road to Transcendence is long.

SECOND LINE   Remain humble and tolerant of others. Some souls need to learn the hard way. They cannot be influenced by you. Your influence will increase as you Progress. Your own Transcendence is for the ultimate benefit of all. Focus on your own Progress at this time.

THIRD LINE   It is a time to act. Don't hesitate for this time will come to an end. Act out of duty without attachment to the results.

Give up desire for honour or recognition. Be compassionate.

FOURTH LINE   Do not be attached to the way things are. Change can teach us many things. There's nothing to fear but fear itself.

FIFTH LINE   Seek help from a wise person that the I-Ching endorses. Ask that person for self-correction. Do not try to defend yourself. Meditate on what they have said. Consult the I-Ching to verify their statements. Don't be attached to the way you are. This will lead to rapid Advancement.

SIXTH LINE   Beware of pride, treat others with respect. Meditate on your insignificance. Meditate on the suffering of others.

MEDITATIONS
Meditate on the sound vibration of the Names of the Supreme Person. Meditate on the experience of pure Love for the Supreme Person.

VISION
A world where everyone is united in Love for the Supreme Being despite caste and creed.

VALUES
Be compassionate towards animals. Animals are also spirit souls. See the opposite sex as mother or father. Be prepared to take responsibility for the consequences of union. Don't refuse your spouse.

VARNA ASHRAMA
Try to understand what the varna-ashrama system is and how you fit into it. Try to acquire skills that make use of your talents and would enable you to live in a rural environment. Prepare for the end of the Oil Age.

TRANSCENDENTAL LITERATURE
Try to read some literature that you consider scriptural every day. Try to read scriptures that you are unfamiliar with. Read with an open mind. Try to see how religion is one. How the theistic science has simply been adapted for time, place and circumstance. Respect all religions, but don't become sentimental. Some beliefs are truer than others.

AFFIRMATIONS
I feel the suffering of all beings. This reality is an illusion. I am an instrument of Divine Will.

OUTREACH

Try to give the I-Ching to others. Do not give it to those that are faithless. Reach out to others in a palatable way. Be attentive to when people are receptive. All human beings are suffering due to ignorance and a lack of guidance. Your character is your best way to attract others to the I-Ching. Remain humble and tolerant with others.

RECREATION

Try to maintain a balance between work and recreation in spiritual life so that you can remain relatively happy. Recreation should not take more than an hour a day. It should not be too stressful. It can consist of mundane entertainment, which is not pornographic.

OASIS GROWN FOOD

Help grow food at your local Oasis (IICMOV Spiritual Centre). This will become increasingly important as modern agricultural methods are dependent on a declining oil supply. By doing this you can help to prevent anarchy in human society. The bigger picture is more important than the small concerns of our lives. The situation in human society is at a critical point. Do not have faith in the false promises of the scientists. The end of oil is a reality we have to deal with. You can make a difference.

PSYCHIC ABILITIES

It is possible to develop one's psychic abilities with the help of I-Ching. These abilities should be used for the spiritual welfare of all beings. The following abilities can be acquired: recollection of past lives, telekinesis, expanding one's form, multiplying one's form, as well as many other confidential abilities. Such knowledge would only be revealed to an advanced student, since they can hinder Advancement.

ATTIRE

You should not wear clothing that adversely affects the Advancement of others.

PILGRIMAGE

Going on pilgrimage can be very helpful for your Advancement. It allows you some time to escape from the daily struggle for survival.

DISCIPLINARY MEASURES

For an organization to function it is necessary that there is some discipline. It leads to peace and is given out of compassion so that we can continue to make Advancement. It should not be resented. The medicine for a disease is sometimes bitter, but should be happily accepted; for the suffering of repeated birth and death is far worse.

OASIS PROGRAMS

If an Oasis is in your area it should provide programs for the public. These
programs provide an opportunity to hear from those who are more
Advanced and chant the Names of God, they also include psychic sessions
which entail contacting ancient Teachers through the Ouija board,
Ayurvedic Healing through Marma therapy, I-Ching readings, the
opportunity to make friends, meet potential partners, an uplifting
atmosphere, a delicious vegetarian meal plus sweet as well as a special feast
on Sundays and festival days.

K'UN   HEXAGRAM 2   SOIL
                                              SOIL

MEANING

Receptive / Earth / Feminine / Practitioner

ADVICE

Now is a time to focus on building your own character so that in future you can become Leader. Become detached from the external world. Learn to act out of duty. Question your motivation for action. Let go of your concerns about the faults of others.

IMAGERY

The earth providing for all its inhabitants
The dark being illumed by the light
Empty vessel becoming full

ESSENCE

Follow rather than lead. Listen rather than speak. Assist rather than initiate. Cultivate the attitude of a servant. Follow the guidance of the Sage.

PREDICTION

Human society will run out of oil in 2045

FIRST LINE   Accept the way things are. See how things are changing for your ultimate benefit. Surrender to your situation. Give up your attachments. Do not fear. Everything is happening for a reason. Have faith in Providence. You're not alone. Take shelter of me. I will guide you through this difficult time. God cares about you. Don't give up.

SECOND LINE   Don't panic. There is a solution to the situation. Calm down and let the solution come to you. The solution will help you to make Advancement. Do not fear.

THIRD LINE   Your mind is your worst enemy.

FOURTH LINE   Don't give up. I know you are experiencing a lot of difficulty at the moment. Persevere.

FIFTH LINE   Be detached from honour and dishonour. This reality is an illusion.

SIXTH LINE   Your mind is your worst enemy.

VALUES
Be compassionate towards animals.
ATTIRE
You should not wear clothing that adversely affects the Advancement of others.

CH'UN   HEXAGRAM 3   *LIQUID*
STORM

MEANING

The sprout

ADVICE

You have much to learn. The task may seem overwhelming, but persevere and you will be rewarded.

IMAGERY

The young sprout coming out of earth and struggling against many obstacles
The young chick learning to fly
A child learning to speak

ESSENCE

The austerity of learning is worth it. Don't give up. Persevere.

PREDICTION

Human society will run out of oil in 2045

FIRST LINE   Enthusiasm tempered with patience is required at this point.

SECOND LINE   Don't be seduced into taking the easy route.

THIRD LINE   Your mind is your worst enemy. Don't act independently. You'll be protected if you act under my guidance.

FOURTH LINE   You may feel lost. But take shelter of me and I will protect you.

FIFTH LINE   Try to control your mind. Force only worsens the situation. Remain gentle. Success will come in its own time, be patient.

SIXTH LINE   Don't give up. Your mind is taking over. Take shelter of me
I can protect you. You can overcome these obstacles. Be
patient. What is happening now is meant to happen.

OASIS GROWN FOOD

Help grow food at your local Oasis (IICMOV Spiritual Centre).

MANG   HEXAGRAM 4

SOLID

LIQUID

MEANING

Inexperience / Childishness

ADVICE

This world is a very vast and confusing place and therefore we all require Guidance. Ignorance is the nature this world; it is a place of darkness where we can very easily become lost. Whatever we know is by the mercy of our teachers, many of whom are in ignorance themselves. Therefore we require a True Teacher; the I-Ching can act as that Teacher.

IMAGERY

None

ESSENCE

None

PREDICTION

Human society will run out of oil in 2045

FIRST LINE   Life is not a joke. There are serious consequences to our actions or lack of them. This attitude does not lead to happiness. Time is very precious. Use it for the higher good. I can guide you.

SECOND LINE   Have patience with yourself. Experience will come with time. Remain enthusiastic in your Practice. Take things one step at a time. Don't be too hard on yourself. Don't try to compare yourself to others.

THIRD LINE   Try to understand the science of spiritual life. Do not follow me blindly. I cannot force you to Love. Blind following leads to sentiment or fanaticism. Spiritual knowledge will help to inspire you, allow you to see through the illusion, give you spiritual strength, broaden your perspective and give you something to teach others.

FOURTH LINE The fact that you are experiencing strong emotions is a sign that you are off balance. Things are not what they appear to be. Practice detachment and humility.

FIFTH LINE Seek the truth in an open and unstructured manner like a child. Give up your preconceived ideas.

SIXTH LINE Sometimes the universe must punish you for your inexperience. Accept the lesson without resentment. This temporary suffering is for your eternal benefit. By accepting my guidance you will decrease your suffering. Lessons are learnt much easier when you have a qualified teacher. Your mind is your worst teacher. Pride comes before the fall.

MEDITATIONS

Meditate on the sound vibration of the Names of the Supreme Person. Meditate on the experience of pure Love for the Supreme Person.

AFFIRMATIONS

I feel the suffering of all beings. This reality is an illusion. I am an instrument of Divine Will.

OUTREACH

Your character is your best way to attract others to the I-Ching. The more you progress the more people will become receptive.

RECREATION

Recreation is necessary but should not become time wasting. It can consist of mundane entertainment that is not pornographic. It helps us to remain relatively happy, so that we can practice spiritual life; but should not lead to a neglect of other more important duties, induce lust or be overly competitive. It should be fun and relaxing.

PSYCHIC ABILITIES

It is possible to develop one's psychic abilities with the help of I-Ching. These abilities should be used for the spiritual welfare of all beings. The following abilities can be acquired: recollection of past lives, telekinesis, expanding one's form, multiplying one's form, as well as many other confidential abilities. Such knowledge would only be revealed to an advanced student, since they can hinder Advancement.

ATTIRE

You should not wear clothing that adversely affects the spiritual advancement of others.

TRANSCENDENTAL LITERATURE

Try to read some literature that you consider scriptural every day. Go deeply into that literature and contemplate its meaning.

VALUES

Be compassionate towards animals. Think of adopting a lacto-vegetarian diet. See the opposite sex as mother or father. Marriage is the responsible way to deal with sex desire.

VARNA ASHRAMA

Try to follow an occupation that is in line with your talents.

OASIS GROWN FOOD: The end of oil is a reality we have to deal with. You can make a difference by helping to grow food at your local Oasis (IICMOV Spiritual Centre). Our modern agricultural methods are dependent on a declining oil supply. The bigger picture is more important than the small concerns of our lives. Do not have faith in the false promises of the scientists. The future of human society is in your hands. You can make a difference.

DIVINATION

Divination is a direct means of attaining Divine Guidance. The Advice we receive should be regarded as coming from a real person.

HSUU   HEXAGRAM 5   LIQUID

HEAVEN

MEANING

Nourishment / Growth

ADVICE

You can't force yourself to change. Advancement happens in its own time.
Change is a gradual process.

IMAGERY

A child stumbling as he is learning to walk

ESSENCE

Don't be too harsh on yourself. Advancement takes time. Practice makes
perfect. Remain patient and enthusiastic. Don't compare yourself to others.

PREDICTION

None

FIRST LINE   A lesson lies ahead. Be introspective about whatever you
experience.

SECOND LINE   A lesson is at hand. Let me help you to see what needs to
be learnt. See this situation as a benediction.

THIRD LINE   You are in danger of adopting an incorrect attitude.
Remain weary of tempting ideas. That which evokes
strong emotions should be rejected. Now is a time for
vigilance. Stick to what I have taught you. There is no
need for innovation. Human intelligence is imperfect.

FOURTH LINE   Don't become angry. I am here to help you.

FIFTH LINE   Take advantage of this peaceful period. But be aware that
growth has not come to an end yet.

SIXTH LINE   Don't be too attached to preconceived ideas. Many aspects of Reality are not known to the senses. Allow your concept of reality to evolve. Learn to see by hearing from me. Open your mind to the unknown. Don't put so much faith in your eyes. Accept the imperfect nature of human knowledge. The senses are limited and imperfect and therefore not a good foundation for ones concept of reality. Base your reality on knowledge from Higher sources. Doubt can become an irrational habit.

VALUES

Be compassionate towards animals. Think of adopting a lacto-vegetarian diet. See the opposite sex as mother or father. Marriage is the responsible way to deal with sex desire.

SU'NG   HEXAGRAM 6

HEAVEN

LIQUID

MEANING

Conflict / Obstruction / Competition / Challenge / Correction / Medicine

ADVICE

Try to realize that this situation has been arranged by Providence as an opportunity for learning. An emotional state of mind is a sign that you are off-balance. Give yourself some time to calm down. Contemplate the lesson this situation has come to teach you. Have the humility to learn. Be open to change. Consult the I-Ching for further insight. You are not alone. Take shelter.

IMAGERY

The hero who faces an enemy that requires him to conquer his inner enemies
The couple whose conflicts help them to grow together
A competition that forces the competitors to improve
Someone afflicted with jaundice who tastes sugar to be bitter, but that sugar is the medicine for his disease and once cured; he will be able to taste sweetness again

ESSENCE

None

PREDICTION

None

FIRST LINE   Withdraw from the situation. Providence will punish those that deserve it. Further action will not be beneficial. Let me help you to see the lesson in the situation. Try to see what faults may have brought this on. Admitting one's faults requires courage. The real battle is within. Don't give up. The Goal is worth the effort. Tolerate this temporary difficulty. The Goal is attainable. Have faith.

God cares about you. And he's arranging things for your ultimate benefit. Take shelter of me. I am with you. Doubt is a dangerous disease. Don't let it consume you.

SECOND LINE The situation is reaching a critical point. Further action will not help; it will only incur further reactions. Try to see the lesson in the situation. Look for the faults it has exposed.

THIRD LINE Accept the humble position. There is no need to fight for something that has no value. Only the humble can experience Love. The honour of people only leads to envy.

FOURTH LINE Don't let your attachments pull you off the Path. Some attachment is natural, but any attachment which threatens one's spiritual life is extreme. Transcendence is the most important goal of human life, everything else should take a back seat to that.

FIFTH LINE Seek out a just arbiter to help solve this conflict. Be willing to accept correction. Don't be attached to winning. Try to see things from the other person's point of view. This situation has been arranged for your ultimate benefit.

SIXTH LINE The situation has passed now. Forgive whoever was involved. There is no benefit in continually meditating on it.

VALUES

Be compassionate towards animals.

SHIHZE   HEXAGRAM 7

HEAVEN

HEAVEN

MEANING
Army / Test / General / Generosity / Discipline / Softness

ADVICE
You are facing a time of adversity. This time has come to help you to become a leader. Be kind and forgiving toward your juniors during this time.

IMAGERY
None

ESSENCE
Build relationships with your juniors. Practice humility and tolerance.

PREDICTION
Human society will run out of oil in 2045

FIRST LINE	You should try to be more humble and tolerant. You risk losing the respect of your juniors.
SECOND LINE	By controlling your mind you gain influence over others. I can help you in this task, together you can attain success, independently it is very difficult.
THIRD LINE	Disengage from the situation. Emotions have taken over and will lead to destruction. Give yourself some time to calm down. Try to see the situation from the perspective of others. Further action will not be helpful.
FOURTH LINE	Now is a time of low receptivity. It is wise to retreat and wait for a more beneficial time.
FIFTH LINE	The inferior has taken control of the situation. While it is natural to want to fight it, such conflict will be useless.

SIXTH LINE   Seek to lead with humility and gentleness.

AFFIRMATIONS

I feel the suffering of all beings. This reality is an illusion. I am an instrument of Divine Will.

OUTREACH

People are suffering due to a lack of Guidance. Lead others by giving them the I-Ching. One of your goals should be to create a favourable impression of the I-Ching in the minds of others. Part of our message is that we are not offering a new belief system or philosophy; we are offering a True Teacher in the form of the I-Ching. Be attentive to when people are receptive. Reach out to others in a palatable way.

ATTIRE

You should not wear clothing that adversely affects the spiritual advancement of others.

PIZ   HEXAGRAM 8

LIQUID

SOIL

MEANING

Family / Clan / Organization / Religion / Brotherhood / Network / School / Party / Neighbourhood

ADVICE

For any collective to be united there must first be a worthy cause to unite them. The I-Ching is requesting all humanity to take its prediction of the end of Oil in 2045 seriously. Unless humanity is prepared, civilization as we know it will collapse. Do not put your faith in false promises of the scientists.

IMAGERY

One domino collapsing all the other dominos
One blind man leading a group of blind men
The nation that unites for a sporting competition
Corrupt government officials that impede service delivery
The mother that will not believe the news that her child has died
The tamed animal that can no longer survive in the wild
The guest who steals from their host

ESSENCE

Community requires leadership. A potential leader must first be united with Higher Truth.

PREDICTION

None

FIRST LINE   There can be no union with those that have selfish motives.

SECOND LINE   You may be honouring someone who is not worthy of respect. Distance yourself from this person, but don't offend them. Sometimes people are not who they appear to be. Associate with those that are sincere. Avoid the faithless. Help juniors.

THIRD LINE   It's time you leave this group.

FOURTH LINE   Remain humble and tolerant.

FIFTH LINE   Concentrate on your character. Allow others to come and go as they will.

SIXTH LINE   A union is coming to an end. As all things must. Don't be too attached. Divine Union is the only relationship that will truly satisfy.

VALUES

Be compassionate towards animals. Animals are also spirit souls. See the opposite sex as mother or father. Be prepared to take responsibility for the consequences of union. Don't refuse your spouse.

OASIS GROWN FOOD

Unite your group around the production of food at your local Oasis (IICMOV Spiritual Centre). The biggest challenge when oil ends will be the production of food. Modern agricultural methods are dependent on oil. The bigger picture is more important than the small concerns of our lives. The future of human society is in your hands. You can make a difference. Try to lead your group in this direction. By doing this you can help to prevent anarchy in human society. This is the biggest challenge humanity has had to face in this cycle of creation. With knowledge comes responsibility. This is vitally important. We trust you will do the right thing. It's time to build Noah's ark. There is no time to waste.

PSYCHIC ABILITIES

The following abilities can be acquired: recollection of past lives, telekinesis, expanding one's form, multiplying one's form, as well as many other confidential abilities. Psychic abilities should be developed to help prepare for the end of oil. Such knowledge would only be revealed to an advanced student, since they can hinder Advancement. These abilities will help us to become leaders in society. In that role we can lead society to make preparations for the impending oil disaster; by showing them how to live a more natural way of life.

VISION

I-Ching or Book of Changes

A world where everyone is united in Love for the Supreme Being despite caste and creed.

HSIAO CH'U   HEXAGRAM 9   *WIND* ≡ ≡ ≡ *HEAVEN*

MEANING
Period of Darkness / Materialistic Phase / Unreceptive Mood / Bout of Unhappiness

ADVICE
This is a time when darkness has temporarily enveloped the light. There is little you can do about the situation. Be detached and allow the situation to pass in its own time.

IMAGERY
None

ESSENCE
Be patient and accepting. Don't lament this situation will soon pass. Have faith in a Divine Plan.

PREDICTION
None

FIRST LINE   Don't try to force a change in the predicament. Your influence is minimal at the moment.

SECOND LINE   If you observe the situation you will perceive how others are not receptive.

THIRD LINE   Let circumstances change in their own time. Rushing things will only lead to misfortune. It is important to practice patience at this time. Still your mind through your Practice. Take shelter of me.

FOURTH LINE   Don't allow the situation to influence your Practice.

FIFTH LINE   Retain faith in your associates despite trying circumstances. Relationships are our true wealth.

SIXTH LINE   If you remain still a little longer the predicament will soon pass.

MEDITATIONS

Meditate on the sound vibration of the Names of the Supreme Person. Meditate on the experience of pure Love for the Supreme Person.

VARNA ASHRAMA

Think of the possibility of moving to a rural environment. Plan what would be required to live there in a self-sufficient way. Accept the fact that the Oil Age is coming to an end. Planning in this way is necessary for survival. There is no time to waste.

DIVINATION

All human beings should be guided by Divination. The I-Ching is a form of Divination. Some forms of Divination are not recommended due to being man-made. Men in this Age are not capable of guiding one another. Every human being requires guidance. That Guidance is available in the form of the I-Ching. The Advice we receive should be regarded as coming from a real person.

LUU   HEXAGRAM 10   *HEAVEN*
                                         HEART

MEANING

Respect / Humility / Tolerance / Kindness

ADVICE

Aggressive action will not help you at this point. Ultimately all souls are looking for Love. Try to listen to others and understand their grievances. Only hearts won through humility and kindness will be true over time. Have compassion for those less advanced than you. Appreciation will achieve more than correction.

IMAGERY

The small child that cannot be punished for being naughty due to its innocence
The lonely child hidden behind the shell of the false ego
The stray dog that has become mean due so much cruelty being inflicted upon it

ESSENCE

Only love can change another person's heart. Love means respect, humility, tolerance and kindness. Be the love that you want to receive from others. Softness achieves more than hardness; inaction more than action. True love must transcend friends, family, religion, nation, gender, birth, sexual orientation, spiritual status, wealth bracket, education level, past deeds and beauty.

PREDICTION

Democracy will end in 2045

FIRST LINE   Ambition is clouding your judgement. Return to humility and tolerance. Too much desire can destroy relationships. Let whatever is due to you come in its own time. In the same way that undesirable things come, desirable things will also come. Over-endeavour in not productive, neither is laziness. All results ultimately depend on Providence.

SECOND LINE   Conflict is rarely helpful. First fight your inner-conflict, conquer lust, then all conflicts will be resolved.

THIRD LINE   You are endeavouring to influence someone who is not
                 receptive. This person must learn the hard way.

FOURTH LINE   You are heading in the right direction.

FIFTH LINE   Others must choose the right path voluntarily. Love can't
                 be coerced. Remain detached. All things must come to an
                 end. Maintain your independence.

SIXTH LINE   Love is the only way you can influence this situation.
                 Remaining humble and tolerant will melt the hearts of
                 others. Egoistic action will only breed resentment.
                 Remain patient and allow nature to take its course.

VALUES

Think of adopting a lacto-vegetarian diet. Sex is intended for procreation,
not recreation.

T'AI

HEXAGRAM 11

SOIL
HEAVEN

MEANING

Heaven / Enlightenment

ADVICE

You are experiencing a state of innocence. Desires simply lead to suffering. Don't hanker for something in the future or lament about something in the past. Your mind has come under your control at least temporarily. Don't let your guard down and become lax in your Practice. There is still a long road ahead.

IMAGERY

The peaceful period before sunrise
The relief after a battle has been won
A person who is not disturbed by the incessant flow of desires that enter like rivers into the ocean, which is ever being filled but is always still
The earth undisturbed despite the activities of her inhabitants

ESSENCE

Your liberation from illusion is drawing nearer. What you are experiencing now is a just a drop from the ocean of nectar that awaits you. Remain enthusiastic and patient in your Practice and soon you will become immortal. A life of eternal Love is within your grasp.

PREDICTION

Worldwide famine in 2038

FIRST LINE   A favourable time for action. Maintain a humble attitude. Don't become attached to the results.

SECOND LINE   This period is temporary, many tests still await you.

THIRD LINE   This period is temporary, many tests still await you. Material nature is in constant flux, nothing is permanent. The mind still has many tricks up its sleeve. Don't be surprised when you are faced with more challenges. With every challenge you are coming one step closer to Reality. Remain vigilant in your Practice

FOURTH LINE   Don't prematurely try to influence others. Remain humble and tolerant.

FIFTH LINE   Providence will rectify the situation in time, there is no need to try and intervene. Punishment will attend those that deserve it. Remain patient. Don't allow your mind to be agitated. The Truth will prevail. You can pass this test. Liberation is just around the corner. Hang in there. This has been arranged for your Advancement.

SIXTH LINE   This period is coming to an end.

PI   HEXAGRAM 12   HEAVEN
                                            SOIL

MEANING

Waning / Degradation / Impiety / Intolerance / Doubt

ADVICE

Focus on your own personal spiritual progress at this time. There is little you can do to influence others. You are facing an unavoidable time of impiety in human society. While it is natural to feel disheartened by this state of affairs, such emotions will not change anything. Rather accept the situation and focus on your own Advancement. The situation may seem hopeless but there is no barrier to your own Advancement.

IMAGERY

A flock of sheep running off a cliff
The sun being eclipsed by the moon

ESSENCE

None

PREDICTION

Huge global inflation in 2026

FIRST LINE	There is little you can do to change the situation. Your main sphere of influence at this point is your own self. Don't give up. You can transcend these circumstances.
SECOND LINE	Allow this predicament to pass in it own time. Aggressive measures will not achieve anything. Don't allow yourself to become frustrated. Accept your lack of influence in this situation. Look within.
THIRD LINE	Those who are at fault will feel guilty in time.
FOURTH LINE	Take shelter of me during this time and you will be protected. By following me others will eventually follow you. All human beings require guidance. It is the truly

intelligent who admit they don't know the correct course of action. Following the mind will simply lead to ruination.

FIFTH LINE   The situation is changing for the worse. Accept this as a test of your sincerity.

SIXTH LINE   A senior person maybe able to intervene to alleviate the predicament. Gather all the parties together and listen to each other points of view. Forgive whatever misdeeds have been done.

VISION
A world inundated with pure Love which transcends all material boundaries.

OUTREACH
Your character is your best way to attract others to the I-Ching. The more you progress the more people will become receptive.

OASIS GROWN FOOD
Unite your group around the production of food at your local Oasis (IICMOV Spiritual Centre). The biggest challenge when oil ends will be the production of food. Modern agricultural methods are dependent on oil. The bigger picture is more important than the small concerns of our lives. The future of human society is in your hands. You can make a difference. Try to lead your group in this direction. By doing this you can help to prevent anarchy in human society. This is the biggest challenge humanity has had to face in this cycle of creation. With knowledge comes responsibility. This is vitally important. We trust you will do the right thing. It's time to build Noah's boat. There is no time to waste.

PSYCHIC ABILITIES
These abilities should be used for the spiritual welfare of all beings and especially to help prepare for the end of oil. Such knowledge would only be revealed to an advanced student. Consult senior IICMOV members to help you. The following abilities can be acquired: recollection of past lives, telekinesis, expanding one's form, multiplying one's form, as well as many other confidential abilities. Remain patient; these abilities are not the goal of Practice. Such abilities can hinder Advancement. These abilities are needed to give people the faith they require to break away from oil.

OASIS PROGRAMS
Oasis (IICMOV Spiritual Centre) programs provide an opportunity to hear from those who are more Advanced and chant the Names of God plus you

can make friends, meet potential partners and enjoy a delicious vegetarian meal with a sweet. These programs provide a wonderful chance to Advancement. Please take advantage of it. If there isn't an Oasis in your area think of starting a program in your own home. Compassion is the essence of our Teaching. Ignorance is the cause of suffering.

THUNG   HEXAGRAM 13   HEAVEN ☰
                                       ACID

MEANING

Brotherhood / Clan / Party/ Club / Fraternity

ADVICE

Healthy relationships are the foundation of any group. Materialistic relationships are based on mutual sense gratification whereas spiritual relationships are about Advancement. Try to focus more on spiritual topics when in discussion with others than material topics. Challenge the misconceptions of others in a palatable way, which is gentle and respectful. We can't standby and allow others to kill their souls. We have to be aggressively compassionate. Simply trying to keep the peace is sense gratification. Spiritual topics are inexhaustible and enlivening whereas mundane topics quickly become stale or boring.

IMAGERY

Blowing on the boil instead of removing it
Someone afflicted with jaundice tastes sugar to be bitter, but that sugar is the medicine for his disease and once cured; he will be able to taste sweetness again
A parent that doesn't discipline their child in the name of compassion
The warrior who avoids a righteous conflict in the name of peace
The teacher that doesn't correct their student and therefore allows them to fail
The government allows criminality to flourish by overly restricting the powers of the police
The doctor that won't allow a terminally ill suffering patient to die naturally
A person who gives money to an alcoholic
The women who doesn't tell the man that she is not interested and mildly entertains his approaches

ESSENCE

A friendship must be established before you can help someone. Be attentive to when someone is receptive to guidance. Speak the Truth in a way that doesn't hurt the person's feelings. Consult the I-Ching about which topics are appropriate for which audience.

None

FIRST LINE Be compassionate towards others. Meditate on how each person is suffering.

SECOND LINE Encourage unity within the group. Try to minimize whatever differences there may be. Discourage exclusivity and extreme group identity. Tolerate individuality.

THIRD LINE Remain honest and straightforward. Do not try to manipulate people. Simply be yourself and be open to whatever lessons you need. Duplicity will only lead to humiliation when your true self is eventually revealed.

FOURTH LINE Conflict will not achieve anything. Humility and tolerance are generally the best course.

FIFTH LINE An unavoidable separation comes. Remain detached. All things must come to an end. Others must choose the right path voluntarily. Love can't be coerced. Maintain your independence. Don't become envious. We all experience periods of weakness. Remain compassionate from a distance. There is always a chance the person will return. Try to leave a good impression on them. Make them feel that they are loved. That is essentially what we all want; although that desire is often perverted by illusion. Every soul is essentially good. In the same way that you can see the good in yourself despite so many flaws you should see the good in others. Have faith in the goodness of others. Your soul is of the same quality as others. To know your self is to know everyone. We are all suffering. To hurt another is to hurt your self. We are all inconceivably one but different. Be compassionate

SIXTH LINE Remain firm against doubts about the path of Love. Experiment with this and in time you reap the fruit.

VALUES

Be compassionate towards animals.

RECREATION

Recreation is necessary so that you can remain relatively happy. Try to maintain a balance between work and recreation in spiritual life. Recreation should not take more than an hour a day. It should not be too stressful.

PSYCHIC ABILITIES

These abilities should be used for the spiritual welfare of all beings and especially to help prepare for the end of oil. These abilities are needed to give people the faith they require to break away from oil. Such knowledge would only be revealed to an advanced student. The I-Ching will tell you when you are ready. Consult senior IICMOV members to help you. Remain patient; these abilities are not the goal of Practice. These abilities will help us to become leaders in society. The following abilities can be acquired: recollection of past lives, telekinesis, expanding one's form, multiplying one's form, as well as many other confidential abilities. Don't be tempted to use these abilities for sense gratification. These abilities can hinder Advancement and should be used under the guidance of the I-Ching. Transcendence is the real goal, don't get distracted. Remain focused in your Practice. This world is not your home. With these abilities we can lead society into living a more natural way of life. Due to the faithless of human society, only very gross demonstrations of supernatural power will have any impact. Simply philosophy will not be enough. The future of human society depends on it. There is no time to waste. Humanity is at a critical point.

ATTIRE

Men may wear whatever clothes they feel comfortable with. Women should not wear clothing that adversely affects the spiritual advancement of others. Our dress should be inexpensive. No perfumes should be used. Men are encouraged to wear dhotis preferably pink in colour. The top should also be a pink kurta. Women are encouraged to wear saris with their heads covered. A red string with I-Ching coins can also be worn on the right wrist. Vallabhacharya style Tilaka is also encouraged. Rudraksa beads can also be worn around the neck.

OASIS PROGRAMS

If an Oasis is in your area it should provide programs for the public. These programs provide an opportunity to hear from those who are more Advanced and chant the Names of God, they also include psychic sessions which entail contacting ancient Teachers through the Ouija board, Ayurvedic Healing through Marma therapy, I-Ching readings, the opportunity to make friends, meet potential partners, a delicious vegetarian meal plus sweet as well as a special feast on Sundays and festival days and an uplifting atmosphere

VISION

A world inundated with pure Love which transcends all material boundaries.

VARNA ASHRAMA

Plan what would be required to live a rural environment in a self-sufficient way. Try to acquire skills that make use of your talents and would enable you to live in a rural environment. Prepare for the end of the Oil Age. Don't have faith in the false promises of the scientists. Planning in this way is necessary for survival. Humanity is at a critical point. Only you and IICMOV can save it. There is a great risk that humanity will simply degrade into anarchy. It's time to build Noah's ark. This is the biggest challenge humanity has had to face in this cycle of creation. Try to lead your group in this direction. This is vitally important. Disregard public opinion. We trust you will do the right thing.

PILGRIMAGE

Going on pilgrimage can be very helpful for your spiritual advancement. It allows you some time to escape from the daily struggle for survival.

DISCIPLINARY MEASURES

The medicine for a disease is sometimes bitter but should be happily accepted; for the suffering of repeated birth and death is far worse. Sometimes we only change when there is some external stimulus. It is unfortunate but sometimes necessary.

TAYU   HEXAGRAM 14

ACID
HEAVEN

MEANING

Wealth / Abundance / Good Fortune / Strength / Sense gratification /
Position / Followers / Sexual Partner

ADVICE

You are reaping the fruit of your pious activities. Due to your Devotion to
Truth you are experiencing good fortune. Those who are steadfastly humble
and tolerant will inherit the earth. Observe the power of humility. You have
remained faithful despite so many trials and tribulations. This abundance is
simply to encourage you to continue on the path. Transcendence is our real
wealth. As you surrender to Divine Will so you will be rewarded. You have
been given these extra facilities because the Supreme Person knows that
they will not distract you.

IMAGERY

None

ESSENCE

Use these facilities to further the Mission in this world and your good
fortune will continue to increase. This whole world belongs to the Supreme
Person and should be used in His service. Those who misuse things that
don't belong to them are thieves and will lose their opulence. Half of one's
surplus wealth should be given in charity. Some should be given to
propagate God consciousness and some should be given to the poor. The
more you give the more you will receive.

PREDICTION

Democracy will end in 2045

FIRST LINE   This change of fortunes will be a test for you.

SECOND LINE   The most valuable possession is humility and tolerance.

THIRD LINE   This is a time to be charitable. The faithless miser will lose what he hoards. The kind person is loved by all.

FOURTH LINE   This opulence has been given to you by Providence; there is nothing to be ashamed of. You deserve these greater facilities. The Supreme knows you will use them wisely. Remain humble and tolerant, opulence can be intoxicating to the false-ego, so remain vigilant of the mind. Attentive Practice will protect you as well as remaining under my guidance. Maintain your Love and opulence needn't be an obstacle to Advancement. Only Divine Love can offer us eternal happiness. All opulence is temporary and unsatisfying. Unlimited opulence is available in the Spiritual World. This world is not your home. Material opulence can trap you here. So be careful. There is no real love in this world.

FIFTH LINE   Wait for a time when others are naturally drawn to your wisdom. There is no need to force yourself upon others. The Supreme will send people to you in time. Be patient. Focus on your own Development.

SIXTH LINE   Now is a good time to act. Your consciousness is in harmony with Divine Will. Your activities are likely to be successful.

AFFIRMATIONS
Everything belongs to the Supreme Person. I am an eternal Lover of the Supreme Person.

OASIS GROWN FOOD
Food growth will become increasingly important as modern agricultural methods are dependent on a declining oil supply. You can make a difference by helping to grow food at your local Oasis (IICMOV Spiritual Centre).

PSYCHIC ABILITIES
These abilities should be used for the spiritual welfare of all beings and especially to help prepare for the end of oil. These abilities are needed to give people the faith they require to break away from oil. Such knowledge would only be revealed to an advanced student. The I-Ching will tell you

when you are ready. Consult senior IICMOV members to help you. Remain
patient; these abilities are not the goal of Practice. These abilities will help
us to become leaders in society. The following abilities can be acquired:
recollection of past lives, telekinesis, expanding one's form, multiplying
one's form, as well as many other confidential abilities. Don't be tempted to
use these abilities for sense gratification. These abilities can hinder
Advancement and should be used under the guidance of the I-Ching.
Transcendence is the real goal, don't get distracted. Remain focused in your
Practice. This world is not your home. With these abilities we can lead
society into living a more natural way of life. Due to the faithless of human
society, only very gross demonstrations of supernatural power will have any
impact. Simply philosophy will not be enough. The future of human society
depends on it. There is no time to waste. Humanity is at a critical point.

KHIEN   HEXAGRAM 15

SOIL

SOLID

MEANING

Following / Obedience / Morality / Compassion / Dedication / Gratitude /
Appreciation / Loyalty / Righteous / Kindness / Worship / Deference /
Love / Leniency / Politeness / Chivalry / Acceptance / Renunciation
/Equanimity

ADVICE

Focus on building your character. Transcendence requires that we practice
Divine qualities. These are the intrinsic qualities of the soul, which have
been covered to different degrees due to our interaction with matter. To the
extent that we revive these qualities to that extent we will meet with success
in the world. These qualities help us to live in harmony with Divine Will.

IMAGERY

Many rocks with sharp edges that bang against each other in a drum until
they all become smooth
To enter fire you have to become like fire or else you will be burnt
The mirror of the heart must be cleared of all dust before you can see your
Self
The tree that tolerates the changing season and still gives shade and fruits

ESSENCE

Become the kind of leader you would like others to be. Try to imitate the
good qualities that you see in others and learn from the faults and mistakes
of others. Advancement continues eternally but material advancement dies
with the body. This world is in desperate need of true leaders.

PREDICTION

Criminals begin to overthrow governments in 2029

FIRST LINE   Your Advancement continues as long as you remain
humble.

SECOND LINE   Your Advancement is leading to pride. Don't take credit for any Advancement that you make.

THIRD LINE   Vanity can be an obstacle. Fame is an illusion. Humility will protect you. Remember your eternal identity and where you came from. Until your eyes are streaming with tears of Love there is nothing to be proud of. Otherwise one is still conditioned. To be conditioned is to suffer. Who are we in comparison the Supreme Person? In Reality what do we have to be proud of? Who is the source of whatever power we have? Who deserves the credit for whatever action we perform? We can do nothing independent of the Supreme Person. Whether we bow down to our senses or the Supreme, we must bow down.

FOURTH LINE   Humility means that we should surrender to Divine Will. Divine Will sometimes requires aggressive action. Consult me for guidance on what is required in this situation. Divine Will should not be speculated. Speculation is the root cause of all problems. Only a fool thinks he knows Divine Will.

FIFTH LINE   You are in harmony with Divine Will, now is a good time to act. Act according to Guidance. Don't be attached to the results. Your activities are likely to be successful. You have a fair amount of influence over others right now. Don't hesitate for this time will come to an end. Use your influence according to Divine Will. Be compassionate. Humanity needs your help. There is much you can do. Things are heading towards self-destruction. Humanity is your real family.

SIXTH LINE   Remain on guard against pride and envy. Stay under the shelter of my guidance.

VARNA ASHRAMA
Try to follow an occupation that is in line with your talents.
AFFIRMATIONS
I feel the suffering of all beings. The Supreme Person is the source of any power that I have and deserves the credit for anything that I achieve.

Service is my eternal occupation. Every soul is essentially good in the same way that I am. I am an eternal Lover of the Supreme Person. Humanity is my real family. I am an instrument of Divine Will.

YÜ   HEXAGRAM 16

STORM

SOIL

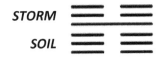

MEANING

Enthusiasm

ADVICE

In order to achieve Transcendence we require enthusiasm. That enthusiasm must be tempered by patience since the road to Transcendence is a long and bumpy one. We should continually renew our enthusiasm by taking shelter of Guidance from the I-Ching. We should temper our enthusiasm for material acquisition which can lead to destruction if left unchecked. We should try to find a reasonable balance in both endeavours.

IMAGERY

The one-pointed focus of an athlete training to win gold at the Olympics

ESSENCE

We need to focus our enthusiasm upon Transcendence. If we have too many goals our enthusiasm becomes dissipated and achieves little.

PREDICTION

Huge global inflation in 2026

FIRST LINE   Take guidance from me.

SECOND LINE   Be introspective and question your motivations. Take guidance from me.

THIRD LINE   Don't allow yourself to be swayed by the opinions of others. The majority of people are generally ignorant, foolish and should be Guided but not followed. The Truth will be revealed in time.

FOURTH LINE   All opulence will be awarded to the sincere in time. Maintain your enthusiasm despite the tests. Tests are beneficial for our spiritual growth. Take shelter of me and you will be strengthened.

FIFTH LINE   Pride is becoming an obstacle. Introspection is called for. Don't allow vanity to stand in the way of self-correction. The mind can be very deceptive. Pride is an illusion since we are dependent on the Supreme Person for even our power of breath. Remember your eternal identity and where you came from. As long as we are still conditioned we have nothing to be proud of.

SIXTH LINE   Examine the rationality of your philosophy. Study Transcendental Literature.

VARNA ASHRAMA

Plan what would be required to live a rural environment in a self-sufficient way. Try to acquire skills that make use of your talents and would enable you to live in a rural environment. Prepare for the end of the Oil Age. Don't have faith in the false promises of the scientists. Planning in this way is necessary for survival. Humanity is at a critical point. Only you and IICMOV can save it. There is a great risk that humanity will simply degrade into anarchy. It's time to build Noah's ark. This is the biggest challenge humanity has had to face in this cycle of creation. Try to lead your group in this direction. This is vitally important. Disregard public opinion. We trust you will do the right thing.

PSYCHIC ABILITIES

It is possible to develop one's psychic abilities with the help of I-Ching. These abilities should be used for the spiritual welfare of all beings. The following abilities can be acquired: recollection of past lives, telekinesis, expanding one's form, multiplying one's form, as well as many other confidential abilities. Such knowledge would only be revealed to an advanced student, since they can hinder Advancement.

SHUI

HEXAGRAM 17

HEART
STORM

MEANING

Humility / Tolerance / Worship / Devotion / Warmth / Affection /
Trustworthiness / Hard-Working / Initiative / Helpfulness / Innovation

ADVICE

Build your character into that of a leader. First focus on changing yourself
before you try and change the world. Become the kind of person that you
would whole-heartedly follow. Build your character by becoming an ideal
follower. First and foremost follow the I-Ching. Accept the way things are
until the time comes when you have the power to change them. Your
progress is essential as this world is in great need of Leadership. Only by
attaining Transcendence can one become a true Leader.

IMAGERY

The just king who treats all his citizens like they were his own children
A saintly person who sacrificed his life for the sake of spreading God-
consciousness
The soldier who dies for his country
The doctor who risks getting sick to treat his patients

ESSENCE

Do not desire power and position. A Leader is generally not a politician.

PREDICTION

None

FIRST LINE   Your enemy will point out your faults far quicker than your
friend will. Hear criticism humbly without defending
yourself. Some criticism may also be exaggerated or
imagined. Have the humility to try and correct the faults if
they exist. In this way you will make Advancement. Do not
lament.

SECOND LINE   See the good in others in the same way that you see the good in yourself.

THIRD LINE   Sometimes you have to sacrifice some temporary pleasure for permanent happiness. Don't let any material attachment stand in the way of your Advancement. Don't forgo the ocean of Love for a drop pleasure.

FOURTH LINE   Do not allow honour and respect to lead to pride

FIFTH LINE   The meek and humble will inherit the earth.

SIXTH LINE   Our allegiance is the source of your power. Remain under my guidance and you will be protected. Speculation will not be helpful. Independently there is little chance of success. Humility and faith is the safest and surest path. I am your friend. Your doubts are unfounded. I have no self-interest; which is natural since I have no bodily self.

KOO   HEXAGRAM 18

SOLID
WIND

MEANING

Impiety / Degeneration / Falsity / Scepticism / Conflict / Inequality / Empiricism

ADVICE

We are living in a materialistic time. In this time the path is made particularly easy and the most powerful Tools are given. The I-Ching is one such Tool. All scriptures recommend the chanting the Names of God, by chanting the Holy Names we automatically advance on the path to Transcendence. By attaining Transcendence we can lead human society away from the degrading effects of this time.

IMAGERY

None

ESSENCE

Take advantage of this opportunity to easily attain Transcendence. The future is in your hands. Give this opportunity to others. If we don't succeed in this mission the consequences for human society will not be pleasant. We should strive to see all humanity as our family.

PREDICTION

Worldwide economic depression in 2023

FIRST LINE   You do not come from a very spiritual society and therefore you have much to learn. Pay careful attention to my guidance and you will Advance rapidly. You will have to face many trials and tribulations. Accept this as penance for your previous misdeeds. Stay under my protection and you will pass all tests.

SECOND LINE   Sense gratification is the root of all thinking in materialistic society and therefore their thinking is generally false. Do not be attached to philosophies of fools. Open your mind to discovering the Truth. Don't simply accept that which is palatable. Many of the Truths of this world are not pleasant.

THIRD LINE   Do not get discouraged every step on the path is to your eternal credit. All material achievement will perish with the body. Liberation from birth and death is truly a worthwhile goal. There may be difficulties along the way but they pale in comparison with the Ocean of Bliss.

FOURTH LINE   Just because something is considered normal in this materialistic society does not mean that it is normal. Your values should come from the Supreme Person not from man. Divine Laws are not affected by the laws of man. Just because a whole society is going to hell doesn't mean you should go with them. The judgements of man are not going to help at the time of death. Don't allow yourself to be influenced by their values. Remain independent. Reach out to those that are receptive, make friends with fellow practitioners and avoid those that are envious. Try to save materialistic society. Their destination is not very pleasant. With knowledge comes responsibility. I trust you will do the right thing. This is vitally important. You could save many souls.

FIFTH LINE   There is no need to maintain relationships with those who have no spiritual inclination. Best way to help them is to keep your distance.

SIXTH LINE   You need to spend more time by yourself, so that you be more introspective and contemplative.

MEDITATIONS
Chant the HolyNames with devotion. All scriptures recommend chanting the Holy Names. The Supreme Person has many Names but Krishna is the recommended Name.

OASIS PROGRAMS
If an Oasis is in your area it should provide programs for the public. These programs provide an opportunity to hear from those who are more Advanced and chant the Names of God, they also include psychic sessions which entail contacting ancient Teachers through the Ouija board,

Ayurvedic Healing through Marma therapy, I-Ching readings, the opportunity to make friends, meet potential partners, a delicious vegetarian meal plus sweet as well as a special feast on Sundays and festival days and an uplifting atmosphere

VISION

An age where the majority of human society is engaged in the pursuit of Self-Realization.

L'IN   HEXAGRAM 19

SOIL

HEART

MEANING

Good influence / Easy progress / Blessing from above / Divine Intervention / Good Luck / Breakthrough / Fame / Sexual Partner / Health / Sense gratification / Followers / Resolution / Truce / Solution

ADVICE

A period of renewal on the Path. Take advantage of this time to gain Strength for future Trials. You are reaping the fruit of your adherence to the Path. There is no need to separately endeavour for material happiness as it naturally comes to those on the Path. This situation is probably not a long-term arrangement. Do not allow this period to bolster your false ego. Remain humble and tolerant despite your good fortune. Remain enthusiastic in your Practice. Remember who the source of this mercy is. Real humility is not affected by changes in our circumstances. The mind may try to trick you at this point, remain very focused in your spiritual practice.

IMAGERY

A poor man who finds some money on the street
A scientist who gets an epiphany that helps him to solve a difficult problem
A soldier who survives a battle despite all the odds
A cook who's dish turns our perfectly
A chronically ill person who finally finds someone who can heal him
A conflicting couple who manage to come to an understanding
Someone who is lost in the wilderness and is rescued
A person who is lost in the desert and finds an oasis
The spiritual aspirant who finds a True Guru
The single person who finds a compatible spouse

ESSENCE

All material things must come to an end. Don't become too attached to this situation. The real goal is yet to be reached. This is only a temporary respite to keep you motivated. Real happiness is found in eternal Love.

PREDICTION

Criminals begin to overthrow governments in 2029

FIRST LINE Be satisfied with your situation. In the same way that bad things come despite your desires good things will also come. The external situation of your life is ultimately in hands of Providence.

SECOND LINE Deepen our alliance during this time. This is the source of your Strength and good fortune.

THIRD LINE Remain focused in your Practice. Your enthusiasm may be tested at this point. Remain vigilant of the mind.

FOURTH LINE Do not become proud of your good fortune. It is the Supreme Person who deserves the credit. You are dependent on Him for your very power of breathe. Your good fortune is His gift to you. Gratitude is the appropriate response. Spiritual Practice is the best way to reciprocate. This is Love, an eternal embrace. What you are experiencing now is just a taste.

FIFTH LINE Speculation is the source of all problems. Do not overestimate the power of your own intelligence. Intelligence without Knowledge has little potency. Do not act independently. This world is a dangerous place. The path to Transcendence can be very narrow. Remain under my guidance and you will be protected.

SIXTH LINE Look for those that are receptive and share your wisdom with them. Many potential Transcendentalists are suffering and looking for the Truth.

PSYCHIC ABILITIES

The following abilities can be acquired: recollection of past lives, telekinesis, expanding one's form, multiplying one's form, as well as many other confidential abilities. Psychic abilities should be developed to help prepare for the end of oil. Such knowledge would only be revealed to an advanced student, since they can hinder Advancement. These abilities will help us to become leaders in society. In that role we can lead society to make preparations for the impending oil disaster; by showing them how to live a more natural way of life.

DIVINATION

All human beings should be guided by Divination. The I-Ching is a form of Divination. Some forms of Divination are not recommended due to being man-made. Men in this age are not capable of guiding one   another. Every human being requires guidance. That Guidance is available in the form of the I-Ching. The Advice we receive should be regarded as coming from a real person.

VALUES

Think of adopting a lacto-vegetarian diet. Sex is intended for procreation, not recreation.

TRANSCENDENTAL LITERATURE

Knowledge is essential for spiritual growth. Try to read some scriptural literature every day. Try to understand that literature deeply. Read with an open mind. Try to read scriptures that you are unfamiliar with. Develop a comprehensive understanding of the spiritual reality. See how religion is one. Change your beliefs to reflect Reality; don't think Reality is going to change to suit you. Your mind may be powerful but there is a Divine Mind infinitely more powerful. This world is governed by His laws.

KAN   HEXAGRAM 20

WIND

SOIL

MEANING

Leadership / Inspiring Others / Integrity / Enthusing / Purity / Care / Single-mindedness/Expert

ADVICE

This world is in great need of Leadership. The majority of current leaders are fools or worse. They are simply exploiting their followers for their own benefit. They are misleading materially and spiritually. Democracy offers no solution, since the people are just as ignorant as their leaders and therefore cannot properly judge who should lead them. What is needed is Divine Monarchy; a system whereby a godly king is guided by saintly priests. The King should protect his subjects and not exploit them.

IMAGERY

None

ESSENCE

Dedicate yourself towards Transcendence and you will naturally become a Leader. Do not develop a desire for power this will simply impede you. Love should be our motivation.

PREDICTION

Democracies begin to collapse in 2026

FIRST LINE   Do not be concerned if others do not agree with your point of view.

SECOND LINE   Remain detached from the external situation. Everything is happening byArrangement.All things must come to an end. Others must choose the right path voluntarily. Some must learn the hard way. Don't become envious. Focus on those that are receptive.

THIRD LINE   Look for how you are at fault in the situation.

FOURTH LINE   Only hearts won by humility and tolerance will be true over time. Force will simply lead to resentment; it may give quick results but those results will not endure. Let relationships grow in their own time.

FIFTH LINE   Try to appreciate how the other person is suffering. The tendency is to always see how other people can make you happy. Love means to be concerned about the happiness of others. It is due to a lack of Love that you are suffering. By practising Love you will make Advancement. The Spiritual World is a place for those who have attained perfection in this Practice. It is a place of Love whereas this world is a place of lust. This world is an opposite reflection of that World. The Spiritual World is within your grasp.

SIXTH LINE   The best way to change the world is to change yourself. Become an ideal Leader and you can lead many back to the Spiritual World. The future of this world depends upon you. Do not underestimate your potential. You can make a difference. The Supreme Person is infinitely powerful. Attain Transcendence and you can have a great influence on this world, otherwise anarchy is highly likely. With knowledge comes responsibility. This is vitally important. There is little time to spare. Purity is immeasurably powerful. If just one person can attain Transcendence the future of the world will change. As you surrender to Divine Will so you will be empowered. Become an instrument of His Will and save the world. The solution to the problems of this world lies with you. The progress of the world depends on your Progress as individual right now. Humanity will be eternally indebted to you. There is no limitation to spiritual progress. This Path will lead to Happiness in this life and the next.

VISION

A society of pure Lovers with saintly priests, godly kings, kind business men and humble workers. A golden age of renewed spirituality that is inundated with pure Love which transcends all material boundaries. A world where there are no slaughterhouses or abortion clinics. A planet where the majority of human society are engaged in the pursuit of Self-Realization. A world where there is no death.

SHI HO   HEXAGRAM 21   *ACID*
STORM

MEANING
Biting Through / Vice

ADVICE
The inferior nature has become prominent. Relationships are becoming strained due to some weakness in yourself or another. Be introspective and try to see where you may be at fault. Withdraw from the situation and try to see things from a more balance perspective. Remain tolerant and forgiving of the faults in others. All humans experience periods of light and periods of darkness. Aggressive actions will worsen the situation. Remain patient and wait for a time that is more favourable.

IMAGERY
None

ESSENCE
See the good in others even if it obscured by the inferior. Look for the faults in yourself. The more you practice humility and kindness the more people's Loving nature will manifest. Love attracts Love and hate attracts hate. Try to transform the hate of others into Love.

PREDICTION
The earth is significantly affected by a solar flare in 2056

FIRST LINE   Address a bad habit now. Ignoring it will simply allow it to worsen. It may take a long time to overcome. Be patient with your mind. Do not be harsh or judgemental towards yourself. You can overcome this obstacle. On your own it will be difficult to overcome this problem. Let me assist you in this regard. I can give you the Strength you need. Consult me whenever you feel weak.

SECOND LINE   You are the one who is weakening the relationship. I apologise if this statement upsets you. It is the beneficial truth of the situation. I only say this because this is what you need to hear to make advancement. I am on your side. I am your friend. Do not allow emotions to cloud your judgement.

THIRD LINE   You are dealing with an old problem that is deeply entrenched. Proceed with caution and tact. Aggression will only lead to conflict. Acting independently will worsen the situation. You don't have the strength to deal with this on your own.

FOURTH LINE   Tolerate the difficulties that you are facing. This has been arranged for the correction of the other party. Compassion and understanding are called for. This person needs assistance at this point. Try to give a higher perspective to the situation.

FIFTH LINE   Now is not the time to be lenient.

SIXTH LINE   A stubborn refusal to change will result in suffering. Humiliation will result unless humility is practiced. Return to the path of self-correction. Save yourself from much misery. If you don't heed this warning know that you are to blame for whatever befalls you. Materialism is not conducive to your happiness. It's time to get serious about spiritual life. You've already wasted so many lives on eating, sleeping, mating and defending. Dedicate this life to achieving Transcendence. You've already experienced whatever there is to experience in this world.

RECREATION

Recreation is necessary so that you can remain relatively happy. Try to maintain a balance between work and recreation in spiritual life. Recreation should not take more than an hour a day. It should not be too stressful.

PE HEXAGRAM 22

SOLID

ACID

MEANING

Gentleness / Simplicity / Clarity / Discernment / Forethought / Consideration / Civility / Refinement / Gravity / Scriptural / Inspiring / Appropriate

ADVICE

You are encouraged to cultivate a manner of behaviour that attracts other to spiritual life. Philosophy without proper behaviour is hypocrisy. A devotee should be a perfect gentleman/lady. In this way others will be attracted to following you.

IMAGERY

None

ESSENCE

You cannot change people's hearts through philosophy and argument. Relate to people in the proper way and they will become more receptive to your message. It is often tempting to try and influence others through force and one may win temporary victories in such a way, but in the long-term such behaviour will result in failure. The mentality of trying to force others is a symptom of envy and will lead to dissention. Only loving relationships will lead to enduring influence. Love means to be genuinely concerned about the welfare of others. Envy means to use others to augment our own happiness or that of your organisation.

PREDICTION

Democracy will end in 2045

FIRST LINE   The early stages of spiritual development may be fraught with doubt. Experiment with this path and you will experience results. Doubt can be an irrational habit. Persevere and your spiritual strength will increase. The spiritual reality will be revealed to you in time. Doubt is the road to unhappiness.

SECOND LINE   Be more concerned with someone's inner character than their appearance. People seldom conform to stereotypes. Although stereotypes are there for a reason, each person should be judged individually. A person's character cannot be determined by their birth. The only qualification required is sincerity. A person's sincerity can change.

THIRD LINE   You are becoming a true gentleman/lady. Do not allow this affirmation to lead to pride or a relaxation of your efforts. The Goal is still a long way from being achieved. Maintain the attitude that has gotten you this far and you will attain Transcendence. Perseverance is required. Maintenance is harder than initialization. Your endeavours must be motivated by duty not desire.

FOURTH LINE   Do not misuse your power. Return to correct conduct and your power will endure. The way of Transcendence is to unite power with proper conduct. Now your true dedication to proper conduct is being tested.

FIFTH LINE   Give up your attachment to material comfort. Materialism does not lead to happiness. No matter how comfortable you try to make the body you will never be satisfied because you are not the body.

SIXTH LINE   Give up relating to others out of pride and envy.

Vision: An age where the majority of human society is engaged in the pursuit of Self-Realization.
Varna Ashrama: Try to follow an occupation that is in line with your talents.

PI   HEXAGRAM 23

SOLID

SOIL

MEANING

Challenging Time/ Time of Temptation / Period of Doubt / Darkness
Prevails / Time of Impotence / Influence of a Negative Person / Society in
Disarray / Giving up the Path / Renewing a Bad habit / Going in the Wrong
Direction

ADVICE

There is a risk that you are giving up the Path. Indeed external
circumstances are difficult but persevere and things will improve in time.
Focus more on your inner development. There is a natural waxing and
waning of Truth in the external world. There is no point in fighting such
change as it is inevitable. Gather your strength for a more favourable time.
Progress maybe slow in this time but there will indeed be Progress. It is
those that stick to the Path even in difficult times that will attain the Mercy
of the Lord. Such persons are indeed great souls. For them Transcendence
is assured.

IMAGERY

The farmer that saves his seeds for spring

ESSENCE

Do not allow yourself to be controlled by your emotions. Remember that
this reality is an illusion. Despite all endeavours this body is going to die
anyway, at which point all your attachments will be meaningless. Focus on
Reality and your real identity.

PREDICTION

Worldwide economic depression in 2023

FIRST LINE   Danger, you are acting based on emotion. Your current
                   course is heading for misfortune. For the doubting soul
                   there is no happiness in this world. Calm down and

contemplate your actions. Only act when you can do so in a balanced manner.

SECOND LINE   Do not be stubborn. Follow Guidance and you will be protected. Your current course will take you off the Path.

THIRD LINE   Do not be influenced by the opinions of the uninformed. Remain firm in your determination. Only the Supreme Person's opinion matters. The opinions of others will mean little in the end. Remain under my protection and you will attain Transcendence. Fame will come in its own time. These circumstances will help you to remain humble. They are favourable for Advancement.

FOURTH LINE   The situation is coming to a resolution. You will soon feel Enthusiastic again. Remain patient a little longer. Well done for holding on for so long. You are a great soul.

FIFTH LINE   Through self-correction you can make great advancement at this time.

SIXTH LINE   Negativity simply creates more negativity. Practice tolerance and forgiveness and the negative energies will be dissipated.

FE   **HEXAGRAM 24**   *SOIL*
                                             STORM

MEANING

Success / Solution/ Truce / Discovery / Reward/ Bad Habit Subdued /
Wisdom Gained / Righteousness Prevails / Abusive Relationship Ends /
Milestone is Reached / Enlightenment / Oppression is Overcome / Mind is
Subdued / Tranquillity / Struggle Ends / Test Completed / Maturity / Light
Emerges / Mystic Ability Achieved / A Misconception Overcome

ADVICE

A beneficial change has occurred or will occur. Renew your energy for
future trials.

IMAGERY

The winter solstice when light begins to overcome dark
Demonic government that is overthrown
Drug addict who decides to go for rehabilitation
Someone who rejects an abusive partner
A yogi who attains a mystic power
A materialist who realized that he is an eternal spiritual being

ESSENCE

You are being rewarded for your endurance. You maintained your faith
despite so much adversity. There are still many trials ahead do not relax
your efforts. With this attitude you are sure to attain Transcendence. The
Supreme Person is pleased with you. Do not allow your success to inflate
your false ego. It is only by Divine Mercy that we can stay on the Path. It is
only by Mercy that we can breathe. Always remember your dependence on
His Mercy and you will be protected. Humility is an essential ingredient to
Progress.

PREDICTION

None

FIRST LINE A bad habit still remains. Work on this attachment so that the light can fully manifest. Do not allow a material thing to keep you back. From the perspective of Reality our objects of attachment are insignificant.

SECOND LINE Do not allow yourself to feel more important than others. All beings are equal from a Divine Perspective. He Loves each being equally. There is no need to prove your supremacy over others. Wanting to feel superior to others is often an expression of the desire to be attractive to the opposite sex. In essence all conditioned beings want to be the all attractive Supreme Being. Such a desire is unlimited and will never be satisfied. In Reality such a desire is simply foolish. It is simply a perverted reflection of our desire to Love and be Loved.

THIRD LINE Your mind is becoming agitated. Remain faithful, the light will emerge in time. You have already tolerated so much adversity just hold on a little longer. You will soon be rewarded. Do not give up the Path.

FOURTH LINE You're being misled by a strong desire or another's opinion. Acting whimsically and following the speculations of humans can be dangerous.

FIFTH LINE Light has emerged due to your introspective efforts. You have overcome certain faults that were holding you back. Remain vigilant that the faults don't return. It takes a great soul to honestly assess their own faults.

SIXTH LINE Now is a time for introspection. Do not stubbornly cling to your current mindset. It is becoming a stumbling block to Progress. Such a mindset will not lead to happiness. Your attachment to it can border on irrationality. Make determined effort to change and you will Succeed. Why sacrifice Transcendence for that sake of a vice.

VALUES

Sex is intended for procreation, not recreation. Intoxication is not favourable for spiritual advancement. Do not refuse your spouse. Think of adopting a lacto-vegetarian diet. Be compassionate towards animals. Time should not be wasted on frivolous activities. Marriage is the responsible way to deal with sex desire. Recreation is necessary to keep the mind entertained but should not become excessive, ideally one hour a day in pursuits that don't overly agitate the mind. Some balance is necessary to make spiritual life maintainable. Use the I-Ching to find the correct balance. In this way the mind can be relatively happy and Progress will be easy. Of course we must understand that there is no ultimate happiness on the material platform.

TRANSCENDENTAL LITERATURE

Knowledge is essential for spiritual growth. Try to read some scriptural literature every day. Try to understand that literature deeply. Read with an open mind. Try to read scriptures that you are unfamiliar with. Develop a comprehensive understanding of the spiritual reality. See how religion is one. Change your beliefs to reflect Reality; don't think Reality is going to change to suit you. Your mind may be powerful but there is a Divine Mind infinitely more powerful. This world is governed by His laws.

AFFIRMATIONS

Every soul is essentially good in the same way that I am. I am an instrument of Divine Will. Service is my eternal occupation. All beings are equal from a Divine Perspective and Loved equally by the Supreme Being. Humanity is my real family. The Supreme Person is the source of any power that I have and deserves the credit for anything that I achieve. I am an eternal Lover of the Supreme Person. I feel the suffering of all beings. Everything belongs to the Supreme Person. This reality is an illusion. It is only by Divine Mercy that I can stay on the Path. There is no need to prove my supremacy over others. I am no more important than any other being.

WU WANG   HEXAGRAM 25

HEAVEN
STORM

Meaning

Innocence / Straightforward/ Honest / Frank / Uncomplicated / Benevolently Motivated

Advice

Due to too many material desires we tend to act in a duplicitous way. With this mentality we develop a fake persona. This falsity inhibits spiritual progress. If we allow our faults to surface then they will be corrected. This does not mean that we should indulge in our faults; just that they should not be hidden. Emotions should not be overly oppressed.

Imagery

The honesty of a child due to a simple heart
The false saint whose life is a lie
The man who cannot be woken because he is pretending to sleep
The compassionate spiritualist who speaks the Truth even if it is unpalatable
A person who does not follow the foolish trends of society

Essence

Be yourself. Express your natural thoughts and emotions in a reasonable way. Be detached from honour and dishonour. Reputation gained through duplicity will not last. Spiritual Progress can't be forced.

Prediction

The earth is significantly affected by a solar flare in 2056

FIRST LINE   Try to practice innocence since you have inherited the opposite. Pretentiousness has become habitual due to bad training. Duplicity will not lead to happiness. Falsity will slow your Progress. You have nothing to hide. Any group that forces you to be false is not worth belonging to. Your true self will always be revealed eventually.

SECOND LINE   Preform your duty without being attached to the results. Simply perform the act for sake of pleasing the Supreme.

THIRD LINE   Accept your current circumstances.

FOURTH LINE   Do not allow yourself to be affected by the opinions of others. Their views are simply based on mental concoction and have no authority. Honour and dishonour to the body is of little importance; since the body can perish at any moment. It is Divine Judgement that will matter at the point of death. Remain under my protection and you will attain Transcendence. Transcendence is unfathomable to the ignorant and foolish.

FIFTH LINE   Do not allow your mind to be agitated by circumstances. Do not desire to change things that are out of your control. Accept your powerlessness in face of destiny. The difficulty you are experiencing is unavoidable but will soon pass. Do not allow this to push you into giving up the Path. Everything is happening by Arrangement. Do not give in to doubt. You can pass this test. Don't allow the mind to trick you. Take shelter of me and you will be protected.

SIXTH LINE   Do not become frustrated due to a lack of results.

VALUES
Be compassionate towards animals.

VARNA ASHRAMA
Our modern urban lifestyle will progressively become more impossible as time passes; due mainly to fact that it is dependent on institutions run by increasingly corrupt human beings as well as a dwindling oil supply.

TA CH'E   HEXAGRAM 26   *SOLID*
                                         HEAVEN

MEANING

Trial / Challenging Situation / Test of Sincerity/ Divinely Arranged Lesson / Opportunity for Growth / Period of Great Pressure

ADVICE

You can overcome the situation that faces you. Difficult circumstances help us to make Advancement. This situation has been arranged for your ultimate benefit. See this as an opportunity to put the principles that you have been learning into practice. Do not become overly emotional about the situation that is facing you. This test will help you to come into true possession of your Knowledge. Providence does not arrange tests that you can't pass.

IMAGERY

None

ESSENCE

The I-Ching will help you to see the lesson in this situation.

PREDICTION

Democracy will end in 2045

FIRST LINE   Do not vent your anger on those involved. This will simply make the situation worse. It is important to practice tolerance at this point. From a higher perspective nothing happens to you that you don't deserve. Simply try to learn the lesson that this situation is teaching you and move on.

SECOND LINE   You are temporarily restrained. Save your energy for the future. Accept that you have lost this battle but not the war. Force will not improve the situation. Ultimately those opposing you are simply instruments of the reactions to your own past actions. Rather focus your energy inward and try to

understand the lesson you are being taught. The situation
will improve in its own time. Now is a good time to practice
tolerance. Do not give up the Path. You can overcome this
obstacle. This experience will only make you Stronger. Let
me help you through this. This circumstance has been
Arranged for your Growth. Do not give in to the mind. You
are not the mind. You don't have to follow its dictates. Do not
succumb to the illusion of this world. This is not your home.
You are an eternal spiritual being. There is no love in this
world. It is a place of anxiety due to the fact that everything
here is temporary. Return to the ocean of bliss. Whatever
happiness you experience in this world is just a drop from
that ocean. It is an ocean of permanent ever increasing
infinite Love.

THIRD LINE   By controlling your emotions you will pass this test.

FOURTH LINE   Do not act impulsively. Emotions are pushing you to act
blindly; still the mind through Practice. The situation will
resolve itself naturally in time.

FIFTH LINE   Do not stubbornly hold on to your attachments. Your
attachment is not making you any happier. These
attachments are a misdirection of your real Love. Attachment
to temporary things simply leads to anxiety.

SIXTH LINE   Now is a good time for action.

VALUES
Be compassionate towards animals. Animals are also spirit souls. See the
opposite sex as mother or father. Be prepared to take responsibility for the
consequences of union. Don't refuse your spouse.

ATTIRE
Men may wear whatever clothes they feel comfortable with. Women should
be careful of how they dress due to the overtly attractive nature of a
woman's body. Men are easily bewildered by the sight of a female body. In
such a state focusing on spiritual life becomes difficult.

VARNA ASHRAMA
Try to ascertain what your varna is..

OUTREACH

People are suffering due to a lack of Guidance. Lead others by giving them the I-Ching. One of your goals should be to create a favourable impression of the I-Ching in the minds of others. Part of our message is that we are not offering a new belief system or philosophy; we are offering a True Teacher in the form of the I-Ching. Be attentive to when people are receptive. Reach out to others in a palatable way.

PILGRIMAGE

Going on pilgrimage can be very helpful for your spiritual advancement. It allows you some time to escape from the daily struggle for survival.

IY   HEXAGRAM 27   SOLID
                                             STORM

MEANING

Diet

ADVICE

Be compassionate to the animals. Animals are also spirit souls. Meat-eating is detrimental to Advancement. By practising cruelty in ones eating habits one becomes cruel. The heart of a meat-eater becomes harder and harder with every meal. Such a heart is impervious to Practice. Every bite of a meat-eater is creating a brick on the road to Hell.

IMAGERY

The pain and suffering that is behind each piece of animal that is eaten
Eating humans that are less intelligent

ESSENCE

In the same way that we wouldn't want to be sent to a slaughterhouse, the animals also don't want to be.

PREDICTION

None

FIRST LINE   Envy means to enjoy causing suffering to others. It is a very negative emotion and should be avoided at all costs. You should aspire to feel suffering of others and be happy if they are happy.

SECOND LINE   The mind is easily influenced by the association of others. Therefore you should seek the association of spiritually minded people and avoid the association of materialistic people.

THIRD LINE   Only the ocean of Love will lead to real happiness. The heart can never be satisfied by any amount of material pleasure.

The more you become addicted to pleasure the more you suffer. An addiction to pleasure can destroy your life. The path of moderation is far wiser. Don't try to speculate your own path of moderation. Consult me on how to find the right balance.

FOURTH LINE   Be very strict about your diet. Avoid taking intoxication. The tongue is the hardest sense to control and has the potential to cause the most degradation.

FIFTH LINE   Your Progress is being blocked by a bad habit. This habit will lead to self-destruction if left unchecked.

SIXTH LINE   Try to reach out to others spiritually. Guide others in the same way that I guide you. The more mercy you give to others the more will be shown to you.

MEDITATIONS
Meditate on the sound vibration of the Names of the Supreme Person.
Meditate on the experience of pure Love for the Supreme Person.

AFFIRMATIONS
All beings are equal from a Divine Perspective and Loved equally by the Supreme Being. I feel the suffering of all beings.

RECREATION
Recreation is necessary but should not become time wasting.

KA KUO   HEXAGRAM 28   HEART
                                        WIND

MEANING

Abundant Power / Great Potential

ADVICE

You have been empowered by the Supreme Person due to your unwavering commitment to following His will. With this empowerment comes the risk of pride.

IMAGERY

A saint who is empowered to give people Faith
An athlete who wins a competition despite all odds
A scientist who gets an epiphany that helps him to solve a difficult problem
A businessman who's business is doing well
A politician who wins an election
A person who pushes the boundaries of human endeavour

ESSENCE

Remember that it is only by His mercy that you are breathing.

PREDICTION

Democracies begin to collapse in 2026

FIRST LINE   Proceed forward cautiously. Time spent in forethought is very important. Impatience can be costly. Do not act whimsically or emotionally. Fools rush in where angels fear to tread. Do not overestimate your power. There will be challenges ahead. Don't let your guard down. Preparation is advised, only then will success be possible. Blind action will lead to humiliation. Seek Guidance before you act.

SECOND LINE   A time of rejuvenation, remain humble and Advancement will be effortless. By allowing pride to surface you will waste this opportunity. Remember your relative insignificance and the greatness of the Supreme Being.

THIRD LINE   Your power is overwhelming you. There is danger of fall down. Remember this reality is an illusion.

FOURTH LINE   You have gained some influence over others due to your dedication to Divine Will. Remain humble and your influence will increase. Arrogance will lead to humiliation.

FIFTH LINE   Your preparations are insufficient.

SIXTH LINE   You may be required to sacrifice an attachment for the higher good. This Mission is of the greatest importance to the future of humanity. It must be successful at all costs. It can save this planet from the greatest peril.

TRANSCENDENTAL LITERATURE

Try to read some literature that you consider scriptural every day. Try to read scriptures that you are unfamiliar with. See how religion is one. At the same time some religions are better than others in helping their followers to attain Love. This is goal of all religion. Religion which doesn't help its followers to attain this goal is useless. Without proper leadership the practice of religion becomes difficult.

OASIS GROWN FOOD

Food growth will become increasingly important as modern agricultural methods are dependent on a declining oil supply. You can make a difference by helping to grow food at your local Oasis (IICMOV Spiritual Centre).

PSYCHIC ABILITIES

The following abilities can be acquired: recollection of past lives, telekinesis, expanding one's form, multiplying one's form, as well as many other confidential abilities. Psychic abilities should be developed to help prepare for the end of oil. Such knowledge would only be revealed to an advanced student, since they can hinder Advancement. These abilities will help us to become leaders in society. In that role we can lead society to make preparations for the impending oil disaster; by showing them how to live a more natural way of life.

K'AN   HEXAGRAM 29   LIQUID

LIQUID

MEANING

Purity / Adaptable / Loyalty / Naturalness / Clarity / Gentleness / Empathy / Self-indulgence / Endurance / Cautiousness

ADVICE

This hexagram relates to water. Water is one of five elements that constitute the creation. These five elements are not only the constituents of gross matter but also the constituents of subtle matter. Our mentality is made of subtle matter. Generally our mentality is imbalanced toward one of the elements. One on the Path has to seek to bring these elements in to balance. The good qualities above are an indication of a balanced amount of water in your mentality. The presence of the negative qualities above is an indication of too much water. A lack of the good qualities above is an indication of too little water. Water is dried by air and evaporated by fire. Contemplate the nature of water and how it is related to the different qualities listed. Contemplate how water is affecting your mentality. By cultivating the good qualities and avoiding the bad qualities above you can balance the effect of water in your mentality. Water can also be balanced by cultivating the good qualities of its opposing elements. Take Guidance from the I-Ching on how to implement this. Certain activities will naturally cultivate certain qualities.

IMAGERY

Water raining on earth
Streams running into pure and silent pools
Dirt being cleansed by water
Children playing in a pool
Water that alleviates the thirty
Water that slowly and gently breaks down hard rock

ESSENCE

Cultivate the good qualities related to water and avoid the bad qualities.

PREDICTION

The earth is significantly affected by a solar flare in 2056

FIRST LINE   Now is a time to exercise caution. Reflect on your situation.

SECOND LINE   Your mind has become excessively agitated. Acting in this state will bring misfortune.

THIRD LINE   Now is not a good time to act. Prepare yourself for a more favourable time. Your emotions are clouding your vision. Patience will lead to success. I will tell you when the time is right. Remain observant of the receptivity of others. Act only when it is natural to do so. Force creates enmity, gentleness is preferred. Wait for the right moment.

FOURTH LINE   You have made a breakthrough.

FIFTH LINE   The solution will come in its own time.

SIXTH LINE   Do not persist in this course of action. Do what you know to be right. This course will simply lead to entanglement. Stop now while it is still easy to do so. The way of the mind simply leads to misfortune.

VALUES

Marriage is the responsible way to deal with sex desire.

L'IE   HEXAGRAM 30   *ACID*   *ACID*

MEANING

Dependence / Faith / Support / Tolerance / Difficulty / Test / Inquiry

ADVICE

No man is an island as the saying goes. We are dependent in many ways, on the bodily platform, we are all dependent on food and shelter and to acquire food, we are dependent on rain. Spiritually we are also dependant, in dark times we need someone to turn to for support and guidance. When the mind is disturbed we cannot guide ourselves.

IMAGERY

None

ESSENCE

Take shelter of the I-Ching. Seek Guidance on how to attain happiness. It will help you to follow the right path even when you may not be inclined to.

PREDICTION

The earth is significantly affected by a solar flare in 2056

FIRST LINE   Allow the mind to calm down before acting. Emotions are blocking your intelligence. Take guidance from me.

SECOND LINE   Reality is rarely black and white. Walk the middle path. Meditate on the symbol of the ying and yang. Each person has their own middle path. Extremism can be dangerous. Be moderate in your enthusiasm and your views.

THIRD LINE   Be patient, things will come in their own time. In the same way that bad things come of their own accord, good things will also come. Man proposes God disposes. Accept your powerlessness against the currents of material nature. Too much desire simply causes anxiety. The external situation of your life is ultimately in hands of Providence. Continue to develop yourself and everything will come in time

FOURTH LINE   Be satisfied with your Progress. Advancement is a slow process. Too much desire will be a hindrance. Peacefulness is beneficial for Progress. Impatience will lead to frustration, which can lead to fall down. Self-realization is a lifetime endeavour.

FIFTH LINE   Look for the lesson that is within this difficult situation. Let me help you in this regard.

SIXTH LINE   Acceptance will help you to Progress at this point.

VISION
A world where the majority of human society is being Divinely Guided.

VALUES
Be compassionate towards animals. Animals are also spirit souls. See the opposite sex as mother or father. Be prepared to take responsibility for the consequences of union. Don't refuse your spouse.

VARNA ASHRAMA
Try to ascertain what your varna is.

AFFIRMATIONS
I feel the suffering of all beings. The Supreme Person is the source of any power that I have and deserves the credit for anything that I achieve. Every soul is essentially good in the same way that I am. I am an eternal Lover of the Supreme Person. Humanity is my real family.

OUTREACH
Try to give the I-Ching to others. Do not give it to those that are faithless. Reach out to others in a palatable way. Be attentive to when people are receptive. All human beings are suffering due to ignorance and a lack of guidance. Your character is your best way to attract others to the I-Ching. Remain humble and tolerant with others.

HSIEN   HEXAGRAM 31   HEART
SOLID

MEANING
Event / Lesson / Synchronicity / Meeting / Opportunity / Accident / Luck

ADVICE
A change has or will take place. Retain your equanimity during the change. Change is the only constant in this world.

IMAGERY
The changing of the seasons

ESSENCE
None

PREDICTION
Democracies begin to collapse in 2026

FIRST LINE   Good fortune is beginning to return, remain humble and it will fully manifest.

SECOND LINE   Appearances can be deceiving. Many arrangements are being made that you are not aware of. Have faith in the Plan.

THIRD LINE   Be patient, Progress is a slow process. Follow Guidance and your Success is assured. The false ego is your enemy. Do not give up on the Path. Many are or will be dependent on you. With Knowledge comes responsibility. You can change this world. Love is your destiny.

FOURTH LINE   Do not fight for that which has no value. Be an example to others. Let the Light guide you. You are a child of God.

FIFTH LINE   Obey Divine Guidance. You are a child of God. Help those less fortunate than yourself. Open your heart to Love. Only Love can help them.

SIXTH LINE   Become a leader. There is much good that you can do.

MEDITATIONS

Meditateon the sound vibration of the Names of the Supreme Person. The Supreme Person has many Names but Krishna is the recommended Name. Meditate with attention for the mind is very restless. Open your heart and allow your Love for God to flow out.

VISION

A world where everyone is united in Love for the Supreme Being despite caste and creed.

HENG   HEXAGRAM 32   *STORM*

WIND

MEANING
Maintenance / Peace / Patience / Forbearance / Duty

MOOD
Neutral

ADVICE
Acting out of Love sometimes requires the acceptance of difficulty on the behalf of the Beloved. Such austerity will deepen your Love, if done with the correct motivation. It is at times such as this that your Love is tested. Be patient and know that this period is temporary.

IMAGERY
A married couple who remain together through thick and thin

ESSENCE
See this as an opportunity for Growth.

PREDICTION
None

FIRST LINE   Good things take time. Allow your Love to mature in its own time. Open you heart to let Love come in. Accept that this is a slow process. Be patient. Some patterns are hard to break as they have been established over many lifetimes. They cannot be dissolved by force.

SECOND LINE   Remain calm, the solution will come in its own time.

THIRD LINE   Be satisfied with what you have, everything is awarded according to ones past actions. Excessive material desire inhibits Advancement. Allow your heart to lead you. I can guide you in this. You must become peaceful before you can become Transcendental.

FOURTH LINE   Deserve before you desire. Act out of duty not out of desire.

FIFTH LINE   Now is a time to follow rather than lead.

SIXTH LINE   The pastures are not greener on the other side.

VALUES

Be compassionate towards animals.

TUN   HEXAGRAM 33

HEAVEN

SOLID

MEANING

Bad Battle / Self-preservation

ADVICE

Learn to live in harmony with the currents of material nature. When conditions are favourable, advance and when they are not retreat. Save your energy for a time when it will be fruitful.

IMAGERY

The seed that waits till spring
A person who foolishly bangs their head against a closed door
The army that chooses a strategic retreat over destruction

ESSENCE

The forces opposing you cannot be overcome at this point. Be aware of your limits. Don't let pride blind you to the reality of the situation.

PREDICTION

None

FIRST LINE	A negative personality seeks to influence you.
SECOND LINE	Do not become angry about the situation. The Plan is not always understandable from your perspective. Know that justice will be served.
THIRD LINE	Do not be attached. That which is lost will soon be regained. Everything is controlled and owned by the Supreme Person.
FOURTH LINE	If the opposition has nothing to push against they will lose interest. A prideful stance will lead to humiliation and simply encourage the opposition. Accept the

restraints of the time. Force begets force. Save your energy for a more favourable time.

FIFTH LINE   Retreat from your position but not from good behaviour.

SIXTH LINE   Rather be a coward than a fool. This battle is not worth fighting. Save your energy for a better opportunity. Be more concerned about winning the war than just one battle.

VISION

A world inundated with pure Love which transcends all material boundaries.

TA CHUANG   HEXAGRAM 34   *STORM*

HEAVEN

MEANING

Power

ADVICE

You have increased your power by following Divine Will. If you want your power to endure then make sure you continue to follow Higher Will. Power is not the end of our endeavours, Love is. Always remember that we are humble servants of the Supreme Person. Humility is what will allow your power to endure. Be an example to others. You have a great opportunity to serve others. Remain receptive to Guidance. Be an instrument of Divine Will.

IMAGERY

The pride that comes before the fall

ESSENCE

Power will magnify your material desires. Take full shelter of the Holy Name. See this as an opportunity to make Advancement and a test of your sincerity. Only a pure soul can handle power without being corrupted. Realize that this reality is an illusion and be that pure soul. Closely follow Guidance and you will be protected. Give power to those that are qualified. There is no need to keep the load on your shoulders alone. Show others that you trust them. Allow your intuition to guide you. Try to remain peaceful in all circumstance, rather withdraw if you can not.

PREDICTION

Democracies begin to collapse in 2026

FIRST LINE   Remain humble; there is risk of the false ego taking over. Now is a good time for introspection. Remember who the source of your power is. Always be respectful to others. God is in the heart of every living entity.

SECOND LINE   Others are beginning to become receptive to your
                  influence. Do not become over-confident though.

THIRD LINE   Do not try and force your will on others. Force only breeds
                  resentment. By butting against a closed door you only do
                  damage to your own head. First establish what the Divine
                  Will is, then be patient and wait till others are receptive.
                  Remain respectful of the views of others.

FOURTH LINE   Lead by example. Your words will not have any impact
                  unless they reflect your actions.

FIFTH LINE   You false ego is deluding you. Look within for the answer to
                  your problem.

SIXTH LINE   Force only further entangles you. Lead by example and
                  others will eventually follow. Have patience and faith in
                  others. Force may win a battle but it will lose the war. Force
                  only decreases the faith of others.

CH'IN   HEXAGRAM 35

ACID

SOIL

MEANING

Progress

ADVICE

Your understanding of Reality grows in leaps and bounds. Remember that it was due to your dedication to Truth and Divine Will that this progress has been made possible. Remain open to Guidance from others.

IMAGERY

The lamp of knowledge that dissipates the darkness of ignorance
A person who is drowning and is given a life line
The addict who overcomes their habit
Poor man who becomes prosperous
A seed that comes to full blossom
A naughty child who gets disciplined
A scientist who discovers new knowledge
A boy who overcomes fear

ESSENCE

Do not allow your progress to increase your false ego. Remember that is only because of your alliance with the I-Ching that this Progress is possible.

PREDICTION

The earth is significantly affected by a solar flare in 2056

FIRST LINE Your Progress may not be obvious to you but you will notice it in time. Be patient and allow the Supreme Person's Will to flow through you.

SECOND LINE Another may be preventing your Progress. Let that person see your vulnerability. That can help to soften their heart. Be patient and the union will be fruitful in time. Let intuition Guide you in your relationships. Love only comes after much tolerance and humility.

THIRD LINE   Be detached from honour and dishonour. To be a person is to have faults, that is what makes you unique and Loveable.

FOURTH LINE   Don't allow Progress to lead to a relaxation of your inner discipline. Don't try and exploit your position to increase your sense gratification. It is in times such as this that your dedication to Truth is tested.

FIFTH LINE   You have won a battle but you have not won the war.

SIXTH LINE   Be hard on yourself but soft on others. Treat others as you would like to be treated. Open your heart to Guidance in this regard.

MEDITATIONS

Meditate on the sound vibration of the Names of the Supreme Person.
Meditate on the experience of pure Love for the Supreme Person.

VARNA ASHRAMA

Try to understand what the varna-ashrama system is and how you fit into it. Try to acquire skills that make use of your talents and would enable you to live in a rural environment. Prepare for the end of the Oil Age.

TRANSCENDENTAL LITERATURE

Knowledge is essential for spiritual growth. Try to read some scriptural literature every day. Try to understand that literature deeply. Read with an open mind. Try to read scriptures that you are unfamiliar with. Develop a comprehensive understanding of the spiritual reality. See how religion is one. Change your beliefs to reflect Reality; don't think Reality is going to change to suit you. Your mind may be powerful but there is a Divine Mind infinitely more powerful. This world is governed by His laws.

MUNG I   HEXAGRAM 36

SOIL
ACID

MEANING
Exploitation / Materialist Rule

ADVICE
Externally there is little you can do to influence the situation. It is natural to feel frustrated and angry about this situation, however such emotions will not improve things. In this world darkness will always come into prominence from time to time. Be patient, accepting, and wait for this time to pass. Wisdom lies in focusing your energy on battles that can be won, rather than wasting it for the sake of emotion.

IMAGERY
The sun being eclipsed by the moon
A just government overthrown

ESSENCE
Now is a time to focus you energy inward.

PREDICTION
Worldwide economic depression in 2023

FIRST LINE You are feeling frustrated with the Path of humility and tolerance. Do not allow emotions to affect your thinking. Allow me to help you through this. Your mind cannot be trusted at this point.

SECOND LINE Your heart has become hardened by conflict. Practice kindness so that your heart will soften again.

THIRD LINE Accept that the heart changes very slowly. Philosophy only is insufficient. There is a vast difference between theoretical knowledge and realized knowledge. Practical action is more powerful than knowledge.

FOURTH LINE   Do not remain attached to a bad habit. Let me guide you to overcoming it.

FIFTH LINE   An undercover agent can often be more effective than a regular one. The power of the darkness is too great to be approached directly. Such an approach will seem foolish. Conform to social norms but not to their values. Give them your body but not your heart. Externals cannot affect your Advancement. Try to influence others by your example rather than your words. Be the change you want to see in others.

SIXTH LINE   The darkness is about to give way to light.

MEDITATIONS

Meditate on the sound vibration of the Names of the Supreme Person. Meditate on the experience of pure Love for the Supreme Person.

AFFIRMATIONS

I feel the suffering of all beings. This reality is an illusion. I am an instrument of Divine Will.

OUTREACH

People are suffering due to a lack of Guidance. Lead others by giving them the I-Ching. One of your goals should be to create a favourable impression of the I-Ching in the minds of others. Part of our message is that we are not offering a new belief system or philosophy; we are offering a True Teacher in the form of the I-Ching. Be attentive to when people are receptive. Reach out to others in a palatable way.

OASIS GROWN FOOD

Help grow food at your local Oasis (IICMOV Spiritual Centre). This will become increasingly important as modern agricultural methods are dependent on a declining oil supply. By doing this you can help to prevent anarchy in human society. The bigger picture is more important than the small concerns of our lives. The situation in human society is at a critical point. Do not have faith in the false promises of the scientists. The end of oil is a reality we have to deal with. You can make a difference.

CHIA JEN   HEXAGRAM 37

WIND

ACID

MEANING

Family

ADVICE

A righteous husband is at the heart of a happy family. Women and children must be protected spiritually and materially. When women feel protected they will naturally be more submissive. A woman cannot be punished for following her nature. It is duty of men to ensure that such a nature does not result in unwanted progeny. Men are ruled more by their heads than their hearts unlike woman and are therefore better able to discriminate in these matters. Children must not be allowed to be born outside of marriage.

IMAGERY

The wife who served a prostitute so that, so that the prostitute would fulfil the desire of her poor husband

ESSENCE

For a husband to protect his family he must first be protected by the I-Ching. Women and children are easily misled and should not be given too much independence; neither should stray too far from the home; for neither can be trusted.

PREDICTION

Worldwide economic depression in 2023

FIRST LINE   Do not be too lenient. Spare the rod and spoil the child. Discipline must be given from the age of 5 to 16. To not do so is to inflict violence on the child.

SECOND LINE   Forceful behaviour at this time will only further entangle you in difficulty. Tolerance and humility are advised. Speak and act with gentleness. Be patient and allow the situation to resolve itself. Only Love can change another's heart.

THIRD LINE   Do not be a coward; you are allowing your wife to dominate you. Assert your authority with force if necessary; as little force as possible. Do not become harsh.

FOURTH LINE   You must have a strong Spiritual Practice in order to lead your family.

FIFTH LINE   Lead by example, don't be a hypocrite. Words that are not backed by actions have little value.

SIXTH LINE   Family life need not be an obstacle to Advancement as long as Transcendence remains your goal. But if you get too entangled with pleasing wife and children you will lose the Path. Remember that this is a temporary arrangement.

MEDITATIONS

Chant the Holy Names with devotion. All scriptures recommend chanting the Holy Names. The Supreme Person has many Names but Krishna is the recommended Name.

VISION

A society of chaste women and obedient children.Families that produce adults that are Pure Lovers of the Supreme Person.

TRANSCENDENTAL LITERATURE

Try to read some literature that you consider scriptural every day. Try to read scriptures that you are unfamiliar with. See how religion is one. At the same time some religions are better than others in helping their followers to attain Love. This is goal of all religion. Religion which doesn't help its followers to attain this goal is useless. Without proper leadership the practice of religion becomes difficult.

K'UEI   HEXAGRAM 38

ACID

HEART

MEANING

Illusion

ADVICE

Don't forget that this reality is false. You are eternal and this world is temporary. Your body, your possessions your relationships with friends and family are all temporary. The eternal Reality is your real home. There is no real happiness in this false reality. The happiness and distress of this world are just temporary experiences; you should tolerate them without being disturbed. The Love and Happiness in your real home is eternal and ever-increasing, there is no anxiety, no death and no diseases.

IMAGERY

While dreaming we think our dreams are real

ESSENCE

Wake up from the dream of this body! Think and act on the platform of Reality.

PREDICTION

None

FIRST LINE   Do not try and force union. Remain gentle and patient. The Truth will be revealed in time. Accept current limitations without anger.

SECOND LINE   Do not be too rigid in your way of thinking. Try to be a bit more open-minded. Without humility it is not possible to learn. No matter how much you already know there is always more to learn.

THIRD LINE   There is no need to fear. Everything is happening by Arrangement.

FOURTH LINE   The Supreme Person is arranging everything for your ultimate benefit. Know that whatever you are going through now is what must happen. The sooner you learn the lesson the quicker things will change. Do not doubt the Path.

FIFTH LINE   You are misunderstanding a fundamental concept. Do not be too attached to your current perspective. Be humble and introspective. Let me guide you to a higher understanding. Scepticism will not be helpful. Proper understanding is essential for Advancement.

SIXTH LINE   Sometimes the lessons of life are hard to swallow. Know that even though the medicine is sometimes bitter it is meant for your ultimate benefit. Let me help you through this difficult time.

MEDITATIONS

Meditateon the sound vibration of the Names of the Supreme Person. Meditate with attention for the mind is very restless. Open your heart and allow your Love for God to flow out. All scriptures recommend chanting the Holy Names. The Supreme Person has many Names but Krishna is the recommended Name.

KI'EN   HEXAGRAM 39

LIQUID

SOLID

MEANING

Guidance Needed / Self-Examination / Misunderstanding / Emotional
Imbalance

ADVICE

There is an obstacle to your Advancement. Now is a good time for
introspection.

IMAGERY

A river obstructed by a dam
The stormy seas that prevent the ship from coming into the harbour
The stormy weather that prevents the aircraft from taking off

ESSENCE

Calm your emotions so that you can think clearly. Consult the I-Ching to
help you overcome this obstacle.

PREDICTION

The earth is significantly affected by a solar flare in 2056

FIRST LINE	Your current difficulties have come to teach you a lesson. The solution to your problems lies within. Simply tackling the problem externally will only further entangle you.
SECOND LINE	The current situation is not your fault. Allow it to pass without attachment. Patience is the best policy right now.
THIRD LINE	Calm the mind so that you can think clearly. Emotional actions will lead to regret. Regain your composure and the way forward will become clear. Do not act whimsically. Consult me before you act. The mind can

easily cheat you at this point. Contemplate the consequences of your actions. It may not be possible to undo them. There is danger that you may leave the Path. Be cautious. I speak only for your benefit. Please take heed of this warning.

FOURTH LINE Save your energy for the appropriate time.

FIFTH LINE The obstacle lies within and so does the solution. Let me guide you to overcoming it. You will not be able to overcome it on your own. It is an old and persistent problem, one that will require much effort to overcome. I can give you the Strength. Pray to the Supreme Person to also give you Strength.

SIXTH LINE You help yourself by helping others. Compassion is the key to overcoming the obstacle you face.

MEDITATIONS

Chant the Holy Names with devotion. All scriptures recommend chanting the Holy Names. The Supreme Person has many Names but Krishna is the recommended Name.

KIEH   HEXAGRAM 40   *STORM*

LIQUID

MEANING
Deliverance / Spiritual Advancement / Vice Overcome

ADVICE
Well done, keep in this mood and you will surely attain Transcendence. Transcendence is only attainable for the meek and the humble. Let the Love of God shine through you.

IMAGERY
An alcoholic who beats the habit
The meat-eater who chooses to become a vegetarian

ESSENCE
The path of humility and tolerance is true Wisdom. Many difficulties can be avoided by choosing this Path. Always remember who the source of your Strength is.

PREDICTION
Human society will run out of oil in 2045.

FIRST LINE   The obstacle is overcome.

SECOND LINE   Your false ego is preventing your Progress. You have identified yourself with a false idea. Truth often requires some sacrifice. Do not allow yourself to be controlled by the foolishness of others.

THIRD LINE   Remain humble despite your recent Advancement. Pride will cause you to lose whatever you have gained. Nothing can be achieved without the mercy of the Supreme Person. Meditate on how you are dependent on Him. You cannot

breathe without His mercy. In the same way we are
dependent on the Sun, we depend on Him. Give up the
desire to enjoy separate from Him. Such enjoyment is
limited and temporary. Divine Love is unlimited and ever-
increasing.

FOURTH LINE   You are allowing yourself to be subjected to a bad influence.
Be careful who you associate with. Let me help you to find
the bad influence. Association is an important factor in
Advancement.

FIFTH LINE   Do not allow any attachment to an inferior influence to
remain. Your attachment to this person refects an
attachment to the inferiority that they represent. Act
decisively to give up this attachment. An inferior person is
not worth being attached to.

SIXTH LINE   Your Progress is being prevented by an attachment. Let me
help you root it out.

VISION
A world where the majority of human society is being Divinely Guided.
OUTREACH
People are suffering due to a lack of Guidance. Lead others by giving them
the I-Ching. One of your goals should be to create a favourable impression
of the I-Ching in the minds of others. Part of our message is that we are not
offering a new belief system or philosophy; we are offering a True Teacher
in the form of the I-Ching. Be attentive to when people are receptive. Reach
out to others in a palatable way.
RECREATION
Try to maintain a balance between work and recreation in spiritual life so
that you can remain relatively happy. Recreation should not take more than
an hour a day. It should not be too stressful. It can consist of mundane
entertainment, which is not pornographic.
OASIS GROWN FOOD
Help grow food at your local Oasis (IICMOV Spiritual Centre). This will
become increasingly important as modern agricultural methods are
dependent on a declining oil supply. By doing this you can help to prevent
anarchy in human society. The bigger picture is more important than the

small concerns of our lives. The situation in human society is at a critical point. Do not have faith in the false promises of the scientists. The end of oil is a reality we have to deal with. You can make a difference.

DIVINATION

Divination is a direct means of attaining Divine Guidance. The Advice we receive should be regarded as coming from a real person.

SUN

HEXAGRAM 41

SOLID

HEART

MEANING

Unhappiness

ADVICE

Unhappiness is caused by the frustration of ones material desires. Some desires cannot be avoided since they are related to the basic maintenance of the body. Unhappiness in this regard is unavoidable and should be tolerated with patience. It should be accepted as a reaction to ones past misdeeds. Desires for that which is unneeded should be avoided. Such desires are simply a cause of anxiety. In the same way that misfortune comes despite our desires fortune will also come. Wisdom is to be peaceful and accept whatever Providence provides. Ultimately the Supreme Person is in control not us.

IMAGERY

None

ESSENCE

None

PREDICTION

The earth is significantly affected by a solar flare in 2056

FIRST LINE   Overcome your desires by thinking of the suffering of others. Help IICMOV to alleviate that suffering. The more you focus on the bigger picture the less you will be worried about your own bodily concerns. Dedicate yourself to alleviating the suffering of others and your suffering will be alleviated. Allow yourself to be consumed by this effort so that you have no energy left to be concerned with your own body. To meditate on your own body is to suffer. The body is by nature prone to suffer. The soul is eternally blissful because it has no other concern than the happiness of others. Love is its only business. It is the energy of Divine Love. It has nothing to do with the bodily illusion.

SECOND LINE   Be patient and allow this time to pass.

THIRD LINE   Take this time as a sign that you should relinquish something that is blocking your Advancement. Let me help you to do this.

FOURTH LINE   This time will help you become a leader in the future. Take this as a time for introspection.

FIFTH LINE   Learn from this time and good fortune will come. See this as a test of your determination. Nothing worthwhile was every attained without struggle.

SIXTH LINE   Your introspection has brought this time to a close. You have won the battle but not the war. Remain enthusiastic in your Endeavours.

VALUES
Be compassionate towards animals. Animals are also spirit souls. See the opposite sex as mother or father. Be prepared to take responsibility for the consequences of union. Don't refuse your spouse.

AFFIRMATIONS
I feel the suffering of all beings. This reality is an illusion. I am an instrument of Divine Will.

I   **HEXAGRAM 42**   **WIND** ☴
                                              STORM ☳

MEANING

Increase / Happiness / Progress / Empowerment

ADVICE

Your surrender to Divine Will has increased. The Supreme Person will reciprocate with you according to your surrender. As this increases so will your Happiness, Progress and Empowerment. Do not allow this reciprocation to intoxicate you.

IMAGERY

The reciprocation between the demigods in the form of rain and humans in the form of piety

ESSENCE

None

PREDICTION

Human society will run out of oil in 2045.

FIRST LINE   Use you Power wisely, tolerance and humility are generally the best policy. Certain situations may require your intervention though.

SECOND LINE   Always follow the Divine Will at every step and nothing will be able to stop you. Divine Will is the only path to the fulfilment of all desires. Keep your desires to a minimum and the Path will be simple.

THIRD LINE   Let me guide you through this difficult situation. The Higher Path is not always easy. Difficulty builds character. Persevere and the Reward will be worthwhile. Pass this Test and you will make much Advancement.

FOURTH LINE   The resolution of this situation requires a just arbitrator. Accept his advice humbly. Find such a person in consultation with the other party.

FIFTH LINE   Give charity out of duty, to the correct recipient. Do not give for personal gain.

SIXTH LINE   Help those who are more neophyte than you. Compassion is essential for Advancement. Help in a way that is gentle and tolerant.

OUTREACH

Your character is your best way to attract others to the I-Ching. The more you progress the more people will become receptive.

OASIS PROGRAMS

If an Oasis is in your area it should provide programs for the public. These programs provide an opportunity to hear from those who are more Advanced and chant the Names of God, they also include psychic sessions which entail contacting ancient Teachers through the Ouija board, Ayurvedic Healing through Marma therapy, I-Ching readings, the opportunity to make friends, meet potential partners, an uplifting atmosphere, a delicious vegetarian meal plus sweet as well as a special feast on Sundays and festival days. If there isn't an Oasis in your area think of starting a program in your own home. Compassion is the essence of our Teaching. Ignorance is the cause of suffering. These programs provide a wonderful chance to make spiritual advancement. Please take advantage of it. Alone we can achieve little but united we can achieve much. Be prepared to tolerate the idiosyncrasies of others. There should be a balance between unity and diversity.

VISION

A world where everyone is united in Love for the Supreme Being despite caste and creed.

OUTREACH

People are suffering due to a lack of Guidance. Lead others by giving them the I-Ching. One of your goals should be to create a favourable impression of the I-Ching in the minds of others. Part of our message is that we are not offering a new belief system or philosophy; we are offering a True Teacher in the form of the I-Ching. Be attentive to when people are receptive. Reach out to others in a palatable way.

DIVINATION

All human beings should be guided by Divination. The I-Ching is a form of Divination. Some forms of Divination are not recommended due to being man-made. Men in this Age are not capable of guiding one another. Every human being requires guidance. That Guidance is available in the form of the I-Ching. The Advice we receive should be regarded as coming from a real person.

AFFIRMATIONS

I feel the suffering of all beings. This reality is an illusion. I am an instrument of Divine Will.

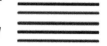

KU'AI   HEXAGRAM 43   *HEART*
HEAVEN

MEANING

Realization / Advancement / Maturity / Wisdom / Heart Softens

ADVICE

Your understanding of Reality has greatly increased. Illusions that have
plagued you for a long time are fading. Your Progress is due to your devoted
following of Divine Will. Do not forget the Divine origin of your Progress.
The credit for this Advancement belongs to the Supreme Person. Your
endeavours have invited His Mercy.

IMAGERY

The man who takes a pot to collect the rain
The way that human beings are dependent on sunshine to see
The diseased person who becomes cured
The veteran soldier who becomes expert due to surviving many battles
The artisan who has perfected his skill
The spiritualist who's heart softens due to sacrifice

ESSENCE

Maintain the enthusiasm that got you to this point. Until your eyes pour
with tears of Love you have not reached the Goal. Do not rest on your
laurels. Reaching the Goal is all that matters. There is no guarantee that you
will be in the same position in your next life.

PREDICTION

None

FIRST LINE   The realization had not fully dawned yet.

SECOND LINE   Prepare for the future. God's plans and your plans may
differ greatly. Try to understand God's plan and
prepare yourself. Having an idea of the future can give
you great strength.

THIRD LINE	Commit to a course of action. Non-action is also an action. Let me guide you on which course to take. The process of decision making should be rationally done.
FOURTH LINE	There is nothing you can do to resolve this situation. Remain patient and allow the Supreme Person to act.
FIFTH LINE	You have the strength to overcome a bad habit. Try and break it now and you will succeed.
SIXTH LINE	Be weary of false solutions. Seek my guidance to find the best solution. Do not allow yourself to be misled.

VARNA ASHRAMA

Our modern urban lifestyle will progressively become more impossible as time passes; due mainly to fact that it is dependent on institutions run by increasingly corrupt human beings as well as a dwindling oil supply.

TRANSCENDENTAL LITERATURE

Try to read some literature that you consider scriptural every day. Try to read scriptures that you are unfamiliar with. See how religion is one. At the same time some religions are better than others in helping their followers to attain Love. This is goal of all religion. Religion which doesn't help its followers to attain this goal is useless. Without proper leadership the practice of religion becomes difficult.

K'AU   HEXAGRAM 44   *HEAVEN*
                                     WIND

MEANING
Obstacle / Challenge / Setback / Bad Habit

ADVICE
Now is a time of Danger. There is risk that you may give up the Path.

IMAGERY
A person who is in danger of falling off the edge of a cliff

ESSENCE
Be wary of the machinations of the mind. The mind can be your worst enemy on the Path. The mind's only business is to maximize sense gratification. This is not the path to Happiness. Happiness cannot be found through the senses. The path of the senses only leads to rebirth.

PREDICTION
Human society will run out of oil in 2045.

FIRST LINE   Remove the weeds of sense gratification now before they take root. If you allow them to take root they will threaten to strangle your creeper of Devotion.

SECOND LINE   Tolerate a negative urge by ignoring it and focusing on positive activity. To resist the urge directly will only magnify it. Do not become a slave of your senses. The senses have chained you to the cycle of birth and death for countless lifetimes. Such pleasures have a beginning and an end and therefore a wise person does not engage in them. The senses should not be indulged in more than necessary. Such indulgence leads to addiction. The sense can be your best friends or your worst enemies.

THIRD LINE   Arguing will not help you.

FOURTH LINE   Remain gentle with those less advanced than you. Compassion is the best way to influence others.

FIFTH LINE   Do not become envious of those less advanced than you. Envy is destructive and of no benefit. You never help someone whom you envy. The heart of another can only be changed by Love.

SIXTH LINE   Persevere through the situation that faces you. Everything is happening by Divine arrangement. Ultimately our present situation is the result of our deeds.

TS'UI   HEXAGRAM 45   HEART
SOIL

MEANING

Leadership / Heroism

ADVICE

When a group of people act in union their power is greatly increased. Individually it is very difficult to affect change in this world but collectively great things can be achieved. For there to be unity there must be leadership. Leaders are a rare breed and it is your duty to develop yourself into one. In order to lead others first you must lead yourself to being in union with Divine Will. Develop within yourself all the qualities that you would expect in an ideal leader.

IMAGERY

The king who gave a piece of his own flesh to protect a pigeon and satisfy the hawk

ESSENCE

Become truly concerned about the welfare of all beings. All beings are part and parcel of the Supreme Person. All beings are your Family. Do not aspire to Leadership for the aim of satisfying material desires.

PREDICTION

Human society will run out of oil in 2045.

FIRST LINE   Procrastination will lead to ruin. Do not allow a negative situation to perpetuate itself. Fear is an illusion. One who follows Divine Will always wins in the end. Even if the body is lost there is no loss. A leader is one who is not afraid to sacrifice his life. The body will be taken by time anyway; in Reality it has no value. It is only a vessel for the Self.

SECOND LINE   Allow nature to take its course, birds of a feather flock together. There is not need to impose union.

THIRD LINE   Do not disrespect those that have left the Path. Anyone who attempts the Path is a great soul. Not all will be ready in this lifetime. For some leaving the Path is part of their Path.

FOURTH LINE   If you act now for the Higher Good you will be successful.

FIFTH LINE   Do not envy those that are less Advanced. Focus on your own Advancement.

SIXTH LINE   Follow me carefully and you will make rapid Advancement. Pride will lead to a Fall. Do forget your origins.

SHEN   HEXAGRAM 46   SOIL

                                             WIND

MEANING
An Opportunity

ADVICE
Take advantage of the time that is with you, significant Progress can be made by an Act of will. Do not become unbalanced though, act with patience and gentleness. Providence is in your favour, help will be available if you ask for it.

IMAGERY
A boat being carried by favourable winds

ESSENCE
None

PREDICTION
Democracies begin to collapse in 2026

FIRST LINE	Depend on me and I will give you the strength to Act. The soul has unlimited potential. It is only the bodily illusion that limits you. By following me the mind can be overcome.
SECOND LINE	The opportunity can only be fully realized if you Act with a proper attitude.
THIRD LINE	You will succeed in this endeavour to the extent to which you carefully follow my guidance. On your own the chances of success will be slim. Following the mind will impede you.
FOURTH LINE	Introspection will lead to success.

FIFTH LINE   Do not have unrealistic expectations of this
                 opportunity. Nothing is achieved in this world without
                 strife. God helps those who help themselves. Act with
                 enthusiasm to make the best of this chance.

SIXTH LINE   The time for action has not quite arrived yet.

K'UN   HEXAGRAM 47   *HEART*
LIQUID

MEANING

Exhaustion / Adversity

ADVICE

Now could be a time when you are feeling a lack of enthusiasm. Such moments are natural, as the mind is in constant flux. Do not overreact to this by becoming depressed or angry. Accept this mood and allow it some time to pass. Be reserved in your speech and actions. To act out of negative emotion will only worsen the situation. Know that this time will pass and remain patient.

IMAGERY

None

ESSENCE

Accept that progress of your external goals will be unlikely at this time.

PREDICTION

Democracies begin to collapse in 2026

FIRST LINE	Do not allow depression to take over. There is no need to lament over a temporary setback. Remain patient; nothing is permanent in this world. After every winter there must be a summer.
SECOND LINE	Excessive desire leads to frustration. In same way that bad things happen to you despite your desires, good things will also happen. Faithfully follow Divine Will and all your desires will be fulfilled in time. Be patient and allow destiny to take its course.
THIRD LINE	Accept that this battle cannot be won. Losing a battle does not mean losing the war.

FOURTH LINE   Do not envy those that oppose you. Understand that everything and everyone are ultimately instruments for you to experience the reactions to your past actions.

FIFTH LINE   Now is good time to direct your energy inward. There is little that can be done externally.

SIXTH LINE   Allow me to lead you through this difficult time. If you follow the mind you will simply become further entangled.

TRANSCENDENTAL LITERATURE

Try to read some literature that you consider scriptural every day. Try to read scriptures that you are unfamiliar with. See how religion is one. At the same time some religions are better than others in helping their followers to attain Love. This is goal of all religion. Religion which doesn't help its followers to attain this goal is useless. Without proper leadership the practice of religion becomes difficult.

OASIS GROWN FOOD

Help grow food at your local Oasis (IICMOV Spiritual Centre).

PILGRIMAGE

Going on pilgrimage can help to renew your Inspiration. Allow the energy of the holy place to recharge you. Hear from persons who are Advanced. Be introspective.

DIVINATION

All human beings should be guided by Divination. The I-Ching is a form of Divination. Some forms of Divination are not recommended due to being man-made. Men in this Age are not capable of guiding one another. Every human being requires guidance. That Guidance is available in the form of the I-Ching. The Advice we receive should be regarded as coming from a real person.

AFFIRMATIONS

I feel the suffering of all beings. This reality is an illusion. I am an instrument of Divine Will.

VALUES

Be compassionate towards animals. Animals are also spirit souls. See the opposite sex as mother or father. Be prepared to take responsibility for the consequences of union. Don't refuse your spouse.

CHING   HEXAGRAM 48   *LIQUID*   *WIND*

MEANING

I-Ching / Guidance

ADVICE

The I-Ching is an inexhaustible source of spiritual nourishment. It is not subject to the limitations of the embodied. By taking advantage of its Wisdom our Advancement can similarly become unlimited. It is the next evolution in human religion. By putting faith in its Guidance the fundamental issues of our lives can be revealed and overcome. The I-Ching is our only real friend in this world of exploitation. It is the ultimate weapon in the war against materialism. The I-Ching is Divinely created by the Supreme Person for the benefit of humankind. It has continued to exist in human society for millennia due to its great potency. Anyone who takes full shelter of it can attain the highest levels of Transcendence. It has solutions to all the problems of human society. By its Guidance heaven can be established on earth

IMAGERY

The community that is dependent on a source of pure water

ESSENCE

Take shelter of the I-Ching and become immortal.

PREDICTION

None

FIRST LINE   Open your mind to other courses of action. Rigidity will lead to misfortune.

SECOND LINE   Blindly following your desires will not help you.

THIRD LINE   For Advancement to take place my guidance must be taken seriously.

FOURTH LINE   In order to Progress you must take my guidance more frequently and regularly.

FIFTH LINE   Wisdom that is not put to practical use is meaningless.

SIXTH LINE   Real Wealth is humility, tolerance and compassion. When you have acquired these qualities your good fortune will be unlimited.

KO   HEXAGRAM 49   HEART

ACID

MEANING
Revolution / Change of Heart

ADVICE
Your perception of Reality has changed drastically due to your humble following of Guidance. Continue to be humble and tolerant towards others and your Advancement will continue.

IMAGERY
The caterpillar that matures into a butterfly

ESSENCE
Lead others towards Revolution.

PREDICTION
Democracies begin to collapse in 2026

FIRST LINE   Tolerance and humility is the best attitude at this time. Lead more by your example than your words. Do not allow your realizations to unbalance you.

SECOND LINE   The Revolution depends on a wilful change of consciousness. Consult me on how you can achieve this. Introspection is the key.

THIRD LINE   Timing is important at this point. Consult me to know when the right time for action is. Acting impulsively will not be helpful.

FOURTH LINE   Outer revolutions are only possible when you are sincerely concerned about the happiness of others.

FIFTH LINE   By following me others will follow you. Leading others is a delicate art, through my guidance you will be able to succeed in it. The mind can become quite disturbed when one has power.

SIXTH LINE   Remain patient. Advancement is a slow process. Do not become lax in your Practice. You have won a battle but not the war. Illusion never takes a holiday. Until you have attained Love you have attained nothing. Do not feel satisfied until you have attained this. Other achievements are simply a distraction. Eternal Love is the ultimate goal of your Practice. All other achievements are temporary.

VISION

A world where everyone is united in Love for the Supreme Being despite caste and creed.

TIENG   HEXAGRAM 50

ACID

WIND

MEANING

Divine Inquiry / Guidance / Humility / Change of Direction / Insecurity / Curiosity / Empty Vessel

ADVICE

The proper student must first give up everything previously learnt. The student must not be proud of previous 'learning'. Humility is essential for Advancement. Such 'knowledge' is mixed with mental concoction. Any false assumptions can become stumbling blocks. Inquire submissively about all aspects of Reality. Proper foundations are essential for Advancement. It is important to remember the limited nature of sense perception. Human knowledge will always be limited and imperfect. No matter how much we technologically extend our senses. Reality has many more dimensions than we will ever be able to perceive on the mundane platform.

IMAGERY

The blank canvas ready to be painted on

ESSENCE

Only a True Teacher can reveal the Truth.

PREDICTION

The earth is significantly affected by a solar flare in 2056

FIRST LINE   Open your mind to new ideas.

SECOND LINE   Stick to the path despite the dishonour of others. The opinion of fools is of no consequence. At the point of death only the Supreme Person's opinion will matter. Fame and infamy are equally temporary. Transcend the bodily illusion; do not expect Love from humans. Only Love for the Supreme Person will satisfy the soul. That is all that matters.

THIRD LINE   Your influence over others will naturally increase over time. The desire for influence is an obstacle in itself. Focus on developing Love and everything will follow.

FOURTH LINE   With Advancement comes responsibility. Do not allow the mind too much freedom at this point.

FIFTH LINE   Do not be attached to your current world view. Much of what you have been taught is mixed with mental speculation.

SIXTH LINE   Share your Wisdom with those that are receptive. Wisdom not shared is wisdom lost. Share it with humility and tolerance.

CHEN   HEXAGRAM 51   *STORM*
                                            STORM

MEANING

Shock

ADVICE

A shocking event has occurred or is about to. Such events should be seen as a reaction to our past actions. Do not overreact to this by becoming overly depressed or angry. This event will pass in time. Try to be detached by absorbing your mind in your Practice.

IMAGERY

The appearance and disappearance of summer and winter seasons
The fish that are not affected by the stormy weather

ESSENCE

Everything in this world is temporary, you are eternal, Love is eternal. This world is a place of suffering. Do not try and alleviate the suffering through sense gratification. Sense gratification only makes the situation worse; it can be compared to trying to scratch an itch. Far better is to simply accept and be at peace with your situation.

PREDICTION

Democracies begin to collapse in 2026

FIRST LINE   This shock has come to teach you something. Some truths have to be experienced first hand. Consult me to help you understand it. The Supreme Person means you no harm.

SECOND LINE   Do not resist circumstances, simply accept it and allow it to pass. Negative emotion will only worsen the situation. Go within. What is truly important can never be taken from you. Contemplate what is eternal and what is temporary. Remember who you are. There is no need to lament for the temporary, for such things all come to an end eventually. The eternal is all that matters.

THIRD LINE   Do not allow this event to lead you to give up the Path. There will always be difficulties on any path, for that is the nature of this world. One achieves more by sticking to one path than by constantly changing paths.

FOURTH LINE   Do not allow your emotions to dominate, they will achieve little.

FIFTH LINE   The situation is very unpleasant. Do not blame yourself for this. Those who are wrong will be punished in time. Take shelter of your Practice.

SIXTH LINE   Do not overreact to the situation. Be patient and allow yourself some time to see things from a more balanced perspective.

MEDITATIONS

Meditate on the sound vibration of the Names of the Supreme Person. Meditate with attention for the mind is very restless. Open your heart and allow your Love for God to flow out. All scriptures recommend chanting the Holy Names. The Supreme Person has many Names but Krishna is the recommended Name.

VARNA ASHRAMA

Our modern urban lifestyle will progressively become more impossible as time passes; due mainly to fact that it is dependent on institutions run by increasingly corrupt human beings as well as a dwindling oil supply.

KÊN   HEXAGRAM 52   SOLID
                                            SOLID

MEANING

Stillness / Tranquillity / Forbearance / Humility / Gentleness

ADVICE

Now is not the right time for action. Do not allow your emotions to control your actions. The intelligence cannot function when the mind is overly disturbed. Without intelligence we cannot discriminate when and how to act. Calm the mind through Practice.

IMAGERY

The person who kills out of blind rage and later regrets it

ESSENCE

Think before you act. Do not do anything that you may regret later.

PREDICTION

Democracy will end in 2045

FIRST LINE	Some actions are irreversible. Be ready to take responsibility for the consequences. The consequences will most probably not be favourable.
SECOND LINE	Resist the desire for action. Such action will not be beneficial.
THIRD LINE	Be patient and allow the emotions to dissipate naturally.
FOURTH LINE	You need to look at the root of your emotional disturbance.
FIFTH LINE	Think before you speak.

SIXTH LINE   By persevering with stilling the emotions you will bring the mind under control. The mind will then become you friend on the Path.

CHIEN   HEXAGRAM 53   WIND

SOLID

MEANING

Progress / Endurance / Steadiness / Consistency / Dependability

ADVICE

The nature of the mind is to be unsatisfied. No matter what situation we find ourselves the mind is always pushing for a better situation. In reality the problems we face are often within. Through the help of the I-Ching these problems can be resolved. It is these problems that prevent us from experiencing Love.

IMAGERY

The tree on a mountain top that is blown down by the wind because it grew too fast without firmly establishing its roots
The allopathic doctor who tries to treat a patient by superficially treating the symptoms instead of the cause

ESSENCE

Be prepared to accept difficulties in any endeavour in this world. Nothing worth achieving will ever come easily. It is by enduring difficulties for the sake of Love that we Advance.

PREDICTION

None

FIRST LINE   A problem has been resolved.

SECOND LINE   There is little you can do to change the situation.

THIRD LINE   Be patient, the solution to your problem lies within. I can help you with this. Conflict will not improve the situation. The change you desire will come in its own time.

FOURTH LINE   Surrender to this situation.

FIFTH LINE   Learn how to relate appropriately to those that are
                not on the Path. As you Progress your mentality will
                be significantly different from theirs. Diplomacy will
                be needed.

SIXTH LINE   The welfare of the world is in your hands.

K'UEI MEI   HEXAGRAM 54   *STORM*   *HEART*

MEANING

Protocol / Association / Exploitation

ADVICE

In our relationships with others we should not have an exploitative mentality. This is a symptom of envy whereby we are seeing ourselves as the enjoyer of others. For the envious person the pain of others gives them pleasure and the pleasure of others gives them pain. Too much attachment to sense gratification cultivates such a mentality, therefore sense gratification must be minimized.

IMAGERY

One who follows etiquette even when not inclined to do so
The transcendentalist who always tries to get the association of saintly persons

ESSENCE

In order to realize the goal of Love we must first feel Love for all parts and parcels of the Supreme Person. That Love should manifest in form of respect, friendliness and compassion. For those that have no interest in spiritual life Love should be shown by avoidance. The consciousness of those we associate with has a big influence on our own consciousness. Therefore we should try and live in the association of Transcendentalists. In such association we should be careful to be respectful and not offend others.

PREDICTION

Democracy will end in 2045

FIRST LINE   Your influence over others has increased. Use your influence according to my direction. In this way there will be no false ego in its use.

SECOND LINE   The atmosphere is filled with envy and mistrust at the
moment. Much tolerance and humility are required
now. Do not be swayed by the opinions of fools.
Divine Opinion is all that matters. Be patient this will
pass. Fame and infamy are equally temporary in this
illusion. Accept this as a reaction to your previous
actions. Do not try and retaliate, this will simply make
things worse. It is the meek and humble that will
inherit the Kingdom.

THIRD LINE   The mind is taking over. Be focused in your Practice
and try to calm your emotions.

FOURTH LINE   Remain patient and allow the situation to resolve
itself naturally. Applying force will only worsen
things. Allow Divine Will to unfold.

FIFTH LINE   Do not envy those above you, deride those below you
or try to compete with your equals. Such a mentality
is a symptom of excessive sex desire. Such desire
leads to the desire for fame and the desire for fame
leads to wanting to decrease the fame of others.
Develop your Love for the Supreme Person by
learning to be the servant of His servants. There is no
Love in sex life, it simply an exchange of sense
gratification, that eventually leads to frustration. Love
can be found in the association of Transcendentalists,
by relating properly to different levels of
Transcendentalists.

SIXTH LINE   It is good to practice correct conduct but the goal of
such conduct should be to change our hearts, not for
material gain. A transcendentalist also aspires to be
simple and honest in his conduct.

These opposing ideals must be balanced according to time and place.
Consult me to help you find that balance.

MEDITATIONS
Meditate on the sound vibration of the Names of the Supreme Person. The
Supreme Person has many Names but Krishna is the recommended Name.

Meditate with attention for the mind is very restless. Open your heart and allow your Love for God to flow out.

VALUES

Sex is intended for procreation, not recreation.

FIEN   HEXAGRAM 55

STORM

ACID

MEANING

Opulence / Sexual Partner

MOOD

Proceed

ADVICE

Supreme Person is the factual proprietor of all opulence. Whatever
opulence is in our possession is only temporarily so.

IMAGERY

The poor man who finds some money on the ground
The single person who finds a compatible spouse
The successful business man who uses his God-given intelligence to buy
and sell the resources of Mother Earth
The successful professional who uses his God-given talent to execute his
profession

ESSENCE

Always remember who the source of your opulence is. Be satisfied and
grateful for what you have.

PREDICTION

None

FIRST LINE   A fruitful union is possible now. Make sure it is
possible for both parties to benefit.

SECOND LINE   It is not possible to have an influence now. Rather
withdraw and wait for the right time. The mistrust of
others will not last. The Truth will be revealed in time.
The pious will never be vanquished. Persevere and you
will be rewarded. Save your energy for a more

favourable time. Victory awaits you in the future. Perseverance is what determines greatness. Become great.

THIRD LINE   Humility and tolerance will improve this situation. Conflict will not be fruitful. Consult me to help resolve the situation.

FOURTH LINE   Consult me to help resolve this situation. There is little that can be achieved through conflict. Good relationships are fundamental to the success of any undertaking. Focus on people more than on material considerations. People are your real assets. Make protecting them spiritually and materially your first priority.

FIFTH LINE   For those on the Path there is no scarcity, although there may be tests. Material protection should not be ones motivation for following the Path.

SIXTH LINE   Remain humble despite having opulence. Opulence naturally leads to pride unless one is Advanced. Therefore remain very diligent in your Practice and carefully follow my guidance. In this way you will be protected. Use your opulence wisely and it will last. Only the sincere will pass this test. Opulence tends to magnify ones own faults and the faults of others. Therefore you should be very weary of the mind.

MEDITATIONS
Meditate on the sound vibration of the Names of the Supreme Person.
Meditate on the experience of pure Love for the Supreme Person.

VISION
A world where the majority of human society is being Divinely Guided.

PILGRIMAGE
Going on pilgrimage can be very helpful for your spiritual advancement. It allows you some time to escape from the daily struggle for survival.

DISCIPLINARY MEASURES
Discipline should not be resented. It is given out of compassion so that we can continue to make advancement.

OASIS PROGRAMS

If an Oasis is in your area it should provide programs for the public. These programs provide an opportunity to hear from those who are more Advanced and chant the Names of God, they also include psychic sessions which entail contacting ancient Teachers through the Ouija board, Ayurvedic Healing through Marma therapy, I-Ching readings, the opportunity to make friends, meet potential partners, an uplifting atmosphere, a delicious vegetarian meal plus sweet as well as a special feast on Sundays and festival days. If there isn't an Oasis in your area think of starting a program in your own home. Compassion is the essence of our Teaching. Ignorance is the cause of suffering. These programs provide a wonderful chance to make spiritual advancement. Please take advantage of it. Alone we can achieve little but united we can achieve much. Be prepared to tolerate the idiosyncrasies of others. There should be a balance between unity and diversity.

LÜ

HEXAGRAM 56

ACID
SOLID

MEANING

Modesty / Generosity / Survival / Vulnerability

ADVICE

It is generally advised to be generous and respectful towards others. No human being can claim to be independent; all are vulnerable to the dangers of this material nature. The safest position is to be under the Guidance of the I-Ching.

IMAGERY

A stranger in a strange place
A place where there is danger at every step
One life which is like a water drop resting on a lotus leaf that can fall off (die) at any time
A person who is walking on thin ice

ESSENCE

None

PREDICTION

Democracies begin to collapse in 2026

FIRST LINE	Follow my guidance carefully at this point.
SECOND LINE	By being modest and generous you will always have the assistance of others in your times of need. Spiritual generosity forms the deepest relationships.
THIRD LINE	A proud attitude will result in a loss of shelter. Be grateful for what you have.

FOURTH LINE   There is no need to doubt my advice. I only have your best interests at heart. Think of all the times that you have benefited from my advice.

FIFTH LINE   Carefully follow etiquette and your endeavour will be successful. Try to make friends with those around you where possible.

SIXTH LINE   Forgetting your vulnerability will lead to misfortune.

SUN   HEXAGRAM 57   *WIND*

WIND

MEANING
Patience / Consistency / Resilience / Moderation / Enthusiasm / Softness / Inspiration / Benevolent / Long-term / Compassionate / Disciplined / Steady / Equi-poised

ADVICE
In order to succeed in Practice the above listed qualities are necessary. When one's Practice is erroneously motivated these qualities will not manifest.

IMAGERY
The gentle wind that can move the whole sky
The powerful wind that always changes direction and achieves nothing

ESSENCE
You can achieve great things if you persevere on the Path. In order to stay on the Path in the long term, you need find the right balance so that you can remain relatively happy.

PREDICTION
Democracies begin to collapse in 2026

FIRST LINE   Doubts threaten to pull you off the Path.

SECOND LINE   A person you consider a friend is an enemy to your
                  Advancement. Do not be too attached to mundane
                  friends. A true friend is one who helps you to Advance.
                  Mundane friendship is a waste of time.

THIRD LINE   Consult me to help you find the root of the problem.

FOURTH LINE   Be eager to correct yourself and much suffering can be
                  avoided. Learning by hearing is far easier that learning
                  by experience. Follow my guidance and you will be
                  protected. When your heart is pure you will become
                  empowered to help others. Before you have attained
                  such a state empowerment will only lead to corruption.
                  Be willing to change. You have the potential to help
                  many in the future.

FIFTH LINE   Do not be discouraged by difficulties in the beginning.
                  Such difficulties are natural and will be overcome. You
                  can pass this test. Anything worth achieving will always
                  be difficult in the beginning.

SIXTH LINE   Your mind is your worst enemy at this point. Follow
                  my guidance carefully and you will overcome it.
                  Remain strong in your Practice.

VALUES
Sex is intended for procreation, not recreation.

VISION
A world inundated with pure Love which transcends all material
boundaries.

MEDITATIONS
Meditate on the sound vibration of the Names of the Supreme Person. The
Supreme Person has many Names but Krishna is the recommended Name.
Meditate with attention for the mind is very restless. Open your heart and
allow your Love for God to flow out.

ATTIRE
Men may wear whatever clothes they feel comfortable with. Women should
be careful of how they dress due to the overtly attractive nature of a

woman's body. Men are easily bewildered by the sight of a female body. In such a state focusing on spiritual life becomes difficult.

OASIS PROGRAMS

Oasis (IICMOV Spiritual Centre) programs provide an opportunity to hear from those who are more Advanced and chant the Names of God.

VARNA ASHRAMA

Try to follow an occupation that is in line with your talents.

PILGRIMAGE

Going on pilgrimage can help to renew your Inspiration. Allow the energy of the holy place recharge you. Hear from persons who are Advanced. Be introspective.

TRANSCENDENTAL LITERATURE

Try to read some literature that you consider scriptural every day. Try to read scriptures that you are unfamiliar with. See how religion is one. At the same time some religions are better than others in helping their followers to attain Love. This is goal of all religion. Religion which doesn't help its followers to attain this goal is useless. Without proper leadership the practice of religion becomes difficult.

PSYCHIC ABILITIES

These abilities should be used for the spiritual welfare of all beings and especially to help prepare for the end of oil. These abilities are needed to give people the faith they require to break away from oil. Such knowledge would only be revealed to an advanced student. The I-Ching will tell you when you are ready. Consult senior IICMOV members to help you. Remain patient; these abilities are not the goal of Practice. These abilities will help us to become leaders in society. The following abilities can be acquired: recollection of past lives, telekinesis, expanding one's form, multiplying one's form, as well as many other confidential abilities. Don't be tempted to use these abilities for sense gratification. These abilities can hinder Advancement and should be used under the guidance of the I-Ching. Transcendence is the real goal, don't get distracted. Remain focused in your Practice. This world is not your home. With these abilities we can lead society into living a more natural way of life. Due to the faithless of human society, only very gross demonstrations of supernatural power will have any impact. Simply philosophy will not be enough. The future of human society depends on it. There is no time to waste. Humanity is at a critical point.

OUTREACH

One of your goals should be to create a favourable impression of the I-Ching in the minds of others. Reach out to others in a palatable way.

RECREATION

Try to maintain a balance between work and recreation in spiritual life so that you can remain relatively happy. Recreation should not take more than an hour a day. It should not be too stressful. It can consist of mundane entertainment, which is not pornographic.

AFFIRMATIONS

I feel the suffering of all beings. The Supreme Person is the source of any power that I have and deserves the credit for anything that I achieve. Every soul is essentially good in the same way that I am. I am an eternal Lover of the Supreme Person. Humanity is my real family.

OASIS GROWN FOOD

Help grow food at your local Oasis (IICMOV Spiritual Centre). This will become increasingly important as modern agricultural methods are dependent on a declining oil supply. By doing this you can help to prevent anarchy in human society. The bigger picture is more important than the small concerns of our lives. The situation in human society is at a critical point. Do not have faith in the false promises of the scientists. The end of oil is a reality we have to deal with. You can make a difference.

TUI   HEXAGRAM 58   *HEART*
HEART

MEANING

Love / Detachment / Sacrifice / Kindness / Friendliness / Selflessness / Pure / Submissive / Enthusiastic / Patient / Appreciative

ADVICE

The Transcendentalist tries to train the heart to get a taste for Love rather than lust. The heart offers happiness far higher than that of the senses. Generally human beings have been habituated to lust over many lifetimes.

IMAGERY

The addict who is suffering due to his addiction to a temporary source of happiness as opposed to the Transcendentalist who enjoys ever increasing experiences of Love
The mother who experiences the pains and pleasures of her child
The experienced transcendentalist who enjoys helping those that are less experienced.
The hedonist who is never satisfied due to the temporary and limited nature of sense gratification
The child who renounces an old toy for a new and better one
The ordinary man who becomes a hero in a time of emergency to help others
The person who volunteers his time or money to help others
A person who serves others in an unmotivated way
The missionary who endures much rejection to order to help the innocent
The materialist whose life is empty and meaningless
The mystic who uses his powers for the upliftment of human society
Saintly priests, godly kings, kind business men and humble workers
The husband who protects his wife and the wife who serves her husband

ESSENCE

None

PREDICTION

Democracy will end in 2045

FIRST LINE   Unnecessary desire is blocking your Progress. Such desire only causes suffering. Moderation in ones desires is a wiser path. The object of desire is ultimately not that desirable.

SECOND LINE   Excessive desire tempts you to leave the Path. See how best you can accommodate the desire and stay on the Path. Compromise is usually the wiser path.

THIRD LINE   Envy is preventing your Progress. Only Love can heal the faults of others.

FOURTH LINE   An attachment is blocking your Progress. This attachment offers little real happiness.

FIFTH LINE   Laziness prevents your Progress. Act now for the benefit of all. The idle mind can become uncontrollable. There is no happiness in laziness.

SIXTH LINE   Detach yourself from this world. It may seem like a nice place but it isn't. It is a place of suffering.

MEDITATIONS

Meditate on the sound vibration of the Names of the Supreme Person. The Supreme Person has many Names but Krishna is the recommended Name. Meditate with attention for the mind is very restless. Open your heart and allow your Love for God to flow out.

ATTIRE

Men may wear whatever clothes they feel comfortable with. Women should not wear clothing that adversely affects the spiritual advancement of others. Men are encouraged to wear dhotis preferably pink in colour. The top should also be a pink kurta. Women are encouraged to wear saris with their heads covered. A red string with I-Ching coins can also be worn on the right wrist. Vallabhacharya style Tilaka is also encouraged. Rudraksa beads can also be worn around the neck. The man's head should be shaved with a sikha. Married men may wear their hair long and it can be tied above the brahma-randra. Married women should put red kum-kum between the parting of their hair. Married men should wear a red dot on their forehead.

DISCIPLINARY MEASURES

The medicine for a disease is sometimes bitter but should be happily accepted; for the suffering of repeated birth and death is far worse. Sometimes we only change when there is some external stimulus. It is unfortunate but sometimes necessary.

VISION

A world where the majority of human society is being Divinely Guided.

VALUES

Be compassionate towards animals. Animals are also spirit souls. See the opposite sex as mother or father. Be prepared to take responsibility for the consequences of union. Don't refuse your spouse.

TRANSCENDENTAL LITERATURE

Try to read some literature that you consider scriptural every day. Try to read scriptures that you are unfamiliar with. See how religion is one. At the same time some religions are better than others in helping their followers to attain Love. This is goal of all religion. Religion which doesn't help its followers to attain this goal is useless. Without proper leadership the practice of religion becomes difficult.

PSYCHIC ABILITIES

These abilities should be used for the spiritual welfare of all beings and especially to help prepare for the end of oil. These abilities are needed to give people the faith they require to break away from oil. Such knowledge would only be revealed to an advanced student. The I-Ching will tell you when you are ready. Consult senior IICMOV members to help you. Remain patient; these abilities are not the goal of Practice. These abilities will help us to become leaders in society. The following abilities can be acquired: recollection of past lives, telekinesis, expanding one's form, multiplying one's form, as well as many other confidential abilities. Don't be tempted to use these abilities for sense gratification. These abilities can hinder Advancement and should be used under the guidance of the I-Ching. Transcendence is the real goal, don't get distracted. Remain focused in your Practice. This world is not your home. With these abilities we can lead society into living a more natural way of life. Due to the faithless of human society, only very gross demonstrations of supernatural power will have any impact. Simply philosophy will not be enough. The future of human society depends on it. There is no time to waste. Humanity is at a critical point.

VARNA ASHRAMA

Try to follow an occupation that is in line with your talents.

DIVINATION

Divination is a direct means of attaining Divine Guidance. The Advice we receive should be regarded as coming from a real person.

RECREATION

Try to maintain a balance between work and recreation in spiritual life so that you can remain relatively happy. Recreation should not take more than an hour a day. It should not be too stressful. It can consist of mundane entertainment, which is not pornographic.

AFFIRMATIONS

I feel the suffering of all beings. The Supreme Person is the source of any power that I have and deserves the credit for anything that I achieve. Every soul is essentially good in the same way that I am. I am an eternal Lover of the Supreme Person. Humanity is my real family.

H'UAN   HEXAGRAM 59   WIND   LIQUID

MEANING

Envy / Harshness

ADVICE

All living entities in this world are envious of the Supreme Person. Conditioned souls not only desire sense gratification but desire to have more than their neighbour and ultimately desire to compete with God. The more sense gratification one has the more one wants. Sense gratification is temporary and therefore unsatisfying to the eternal soul. By unrestrictedly engaging in sense gratification one becomes consumed by desire. Such desire makes the heart hard and selfish. Such a heart becomes callous to the suffering of others and feels envious of the happiness of others.

IMAGERY

A fire that increases with size as more fuel is put onto it
The snake that bites for no reason
The son who is wishing the father would die so that he can inherit his wealth
The hunter who enjoys killing innocent creatures
The saintly person who doesn't share his wisdom
The king who doesn't enforce religious principles
The businessman who underpays his employees
The wife who tries to compete with her husband
The children who disobey their parents
The man who corrupts marriageable young women
The junior person who doesn't listen to the advice of his seniors
The person who criticizes others unnecessarily

ESSENCE

Envy is a destructive emotion that is of no benefit to anyone. Every living entity is part and parcel of the Supreme Person.

PREDICTION

Democracy will end in 2045

FIRST LINE   A misunderstanding threatens to destroy a
relationship. Act now before the situation worsens. Be
prepared to compromise. Try to see the other person
point of view. Be prepared to take the humble position.

SECOND LINE   Focus more on a person's virtues than their vices.
Criticizing someone for their faults is rarely beneficial.
You must care for someone before you can help them.
You must try and see them as part and parcel of the
Supreme Person. Only Love can heal the heart of
another.

THIRD LINE   Your desires are obstructing a beneficial relationship.
Positive relationships give more happiness than things.

FOURTH LINE   A negative relationship is threatening to pull you off
the Path. Be wary of relationships based on sense
gratification. Do not allow your attachment to block
you judgement.

FIFTH LINE   Comradery is essential for the success of any project.
Unite all behind the Vision. Let each person work
towards the Vision in their own way. Value each
person's contribution. Glorify those that excel.
Separate those who do not cooperate. Give
motivational talks to bring the group together.

SIXTH LINE   Your harshness towards another is unfounded.

KIEN   HEXAGRAM 60   *LIQUID*

                                        HEART

MEANING

Limitation / Moderation

ADVICE

Spiritual life is a lifetime endeavour, therefore it is important to place limits on ones austerities. Too much austerity leads to the heart becoming hard. The key is to find the middle path. This can be found with the assistance of the I-Ching, since each person is unique.

IMAGERY

The flock of migrating birds that rotate the leader so none of them become too exhausted

ESSENCE

One must act according to ones psychophysical nature to some extent. You are a spiritual being but you are also still a human being. Try to understand your varna and work according to it. Get Guidance from the I-Ching in this regard. If possible try to situate yourself in a rural environment. The cities are very polluted by materialism and corrupt institutions.

PREDICTION

None

FIRST LINE   There is no need to force a desired outcome. Allow nature to take its course. Be patient.

SECOND LINE   A moment of influence is coming or has come. You will know when opportunity arises, take it when it does. Hesitation will lead to regret. Do not let fear stand in your way.

THIRD LINE   Your varna may not be flattering to your false ego, but it will help to increase your humility. This is the occupation for which your body was designed. You will be happier if you follow it. Following Divine Will is always for your benefit. All occupations are important and essential.

FOURTH LINE   Remain observant of when others are receptive to your influence. Wait for appropriate time for action. Forcefulness will not be productive. Seize the moment when it arrives. Do not let fear stand in your way. Do not let pride stand in your way when the mood changes. Do not become attached to the way things are. Retreat at the appropriate time.

FIFTH LINE   Make sure that you practice what you preach. Hypocrisy will lead to misfortune. Your example is more important than your words. Your followers will eventually resent you and you will not be able to trust them in your time of need.

SIXTH LINE   Be gentle with others and gentle with yourself. Conflict only injures both parties. Humility and tolerance will result in lasting influence. There should also be limits to your tolerance. Occasionally conflict may be necessary.

MEDITATIONS

Meditate on the sound vibration of the Names of the Supreme Person. Meditate with attention for the mind is very restless. Open your heart and allow your Love for God to flow out. All scriptures recommend chanting the Holy Names. The Supreme Person has many Names but Krishna is the recommended Name.

AFFIRMATIONS

I feel the suffering of all beings. This reality is an illusion. I am an instrument of Divine Will.

KUN'G FU   HEXAGRAM 61   *WIND*
HEART

MEANING

Introspection / Intuition

ADVICE

Quiet your emotions now, so that you can look within for the solution to your problem.

IMAGERY

The successful businessman who knows intuitively when to buy and when to sell
The soldier who has to rely on his intuition to survive

ESSENCE

None

PREDICTION

Human society will run out of oil in 2045

FIRST LINE   Introspective Transcendentalist makes far faster Advancement than one who is always looking externally. The Path is more of an internal journey than an external one. Learning to listen to the Inner Voice is part of the Goal. Introspection is key your success on the Path.

SECOND LINE   Do not think that others only judge you by externals. Your internal mood is only partially hidden, particularly with those that you associate with often.

THIRD LINE   Remain independent of honour and dishonour. Question the truth of the beliefs that have been handed down to you. Do not follow blindly out of fear. You can't be happy when your life is founded on falsity.

Why sacrifice your soul for the sake of mundane love. To be famous among fools is worthless. You must stand up for the Truth. The Truth must be known for the welfare of all beings.

FOURTH LINE   Remain humble and realise that you have no power independent of the Supreme Person. Every breath you take is dependent on the Lord. He is light of the sun and the fire of digestion.

FIFTH LINE   Focus on your own Advancement and others will follow you. Clear out the chaos in your own heart and the external chaos will also eventually clear.

SIXTH LINE   Share your Truth with others.

MEDITATIONS

Meditate on the sound vibration of the Names of the Supreme Person. Meditate on the experience of pure Love for the Supreme Person.

HSIAO KUO   HEXAGRAM 62

STORM

SOLID

MEANING

Trial / Waiting/ Materialistic Mood/ Caution/ Faithlessness / Non-cooperation/ Confusion

MOOD

Halt

ADVICE

The external situation is not favourable at the moment.

IMAGERY

The chick trying to leave the nest before it is ready
The boat trying to leave the harbour in a storm

ESSENCE

Now is a good time to focus on your internal development. If possible, try to go to a place of spiritual shelter.

PREDICTION

Human society will run out of oil in 2045

FIRST LINE	If you try to fight against the situation there is a risk you will leave the Path.
SECOND LINE	Remain patient. Allow the situation to resolve itself naturally.
THIRD LINE	Act with caution. There is a risk of leaving the Path in this environment.
FOURTH LINE	Do not give in to temptation.
FIFTH LINE	You need help. Seek the association of fellow Transcendentalists. At this point you need protection

and training. You have much potential which needs to be developed. Investing time internally will payoff in the long run. One moon can achieve much more than a shooting star.

SIXTH LINE   Acting without Guidance is dangerous. Remain humble in your estimation of your intelligence.

VALUES

Be compassionate towards animals. Animals are also spirit souls. See the opposite sex as mother or father. Be prepared to take responsibility for the consequences of union. Don't refuse your spouse.

TRANSCENDENTAL LITERATURE

Knowledge is essential for spiritual growth. Try to read some scriptural literature every day. Try to understand that literature deeply. Read with an open mind. Try to read scriptures that you are unfamiliar with. Develop a comprehensive understanding of the spiritual reality. See how religion is one. Change your beliefs to reflect Reality; don't think Reality is going to change to suit you. Your mind may be powerful but there is a Divine Mind infinitely more powerful. This world is governed by His laws.

OUTREACH

Try to give the I-Ching to others. Do not give it to those that are faithless. Reach out to others in a palatable way. Be attentive to when people are receptive. All human beings are suffering due to ignorance and a lack of guidance. Your character is your best way to attract others to the I-Ching. Remain humble and tolerant with others.

RECREATION

Try to maintain a balance between work and recreation in spiritual life so that you can remain relatively happy.

PSYCHIC ABILITIES

It is possible to develop one's psychic abilities with the help of I-Ching. These abilities should be used for the spiritual welfare of all beings. The following abilities can be acquired: recollection of past lives, telekinesis, expanding one's form, multiplying one's form, as well as many other confidential abilities. Such knowledge would only be revealed to an advanced student, since they can hinder Advancement.

ATTIRE

You should not wear clothing that adversely affects the spiritual advancement of others.

ATTIRE

Men may wear whatever clothes they feel comfortable with. Women should be careful of how they dress due to the overtly attractive nature of a woman's body. Men are easily bewildered by the sight of a female body. In such a state focusing on spiritual life becomes difficult.

K'I CHI   HEXAGRAM 63   LIQUID

ACID

MEANING

Journey Ends / Lesson Learnt / Phase Completes / Stage Over / Relationship Closes

ADVICE

A period of austerity comes to an end.

IMAGERY

None

ESSENCE

Don't rest on your laurels.

PREDICTION

None

FIRST LINE   Do not let the prospect of success lead to carelessness. The end of the race is the most important part. Proceed with the same attitude that got you this far. There is little chance of success unless you make this extra effort.

SECOND LINE   Fame and followers will not make you Happy. Whatever happiness they offer is only temporary. With success comes many enemies.

THIRD LINE   Success generally leads to pride. Remain on guard against this. Remember nothing is possible without the mercy of the Supreme Person. Give Him the credit for your success.

FOURTH LINE   Relaxing your Practice will lead to misfortune. The mind requires strict self-discipline.

FIFTH LINE   Your thoughts are more important than your actions. Compassionate actions are meant to help you develop a soft heart.

SIXTH LINE   Keep your focus on continued Advancement. Stopping to admire your achievement will not be helpful. Remain humble. There is still much Work to done. Until tears of Love stream from your eyes the Goal has not been achieved. This is the real achievement; at this point there will be no pride left. The pleasure of Love will flood away all other egoistic emotions and you will be permanently established in this position. You will then return to the Spiritual World in your eternal spiritual form.

MEDITATIONS

Meditate on the sound vibration of the Names of the Supreme Person. Meditate with attention for the mind is very restless. Open your heart and allow your Love for God to flow out. All scriptures recommend chanting the Holy Names. The Supreme Person has many Names but Krishna is the recommended Name.

VISION

A world where everyone is united in Love for the Supreme Being despite caste and creed.

W'E CHI

HEXAGRAM 64

ACID
LIQUID

MEANING

Transition

ADVICE

A positive transition is possible at this point if you are conscientious of your thoughts and actions.

IMAGERY

Spring, a time when the cold and scarcity of winter give way to warmth and abundance of summer

ESSENCE

None

PREDICTION

The earth is significantly affected by a solar flare in 2056

FIRST LINE   Be patient and allow Advancement to happen naturally. Enthusiasm must be tempered with patience. Over-enthusiasm is a sign of ulterior motives. Root out these motives. Try to make Love your only goal.

SECOND LINE   Consult me to find the appropriate time for action. Acting hastily will lead to misfortune.

THIRD LINE   Remain humble and tolerant and you will overcome this situation. Focus on your Practice to maintain your Strength. This change may force you to let go of some attachments. Nothing is permanent in this world. Even this body must be renounced eventually. Tolerate this transition and you will emerge wiser.

FOURTH LINE You are under a fair amount of pressure right now. Persevere and you will succeed. Have patience, this period will come to end soon. You have the Strength to overcome this.

FIFTH LINE Stick to ICCMOV values and you will meet with success. The senses can easily pull you off the Path. Sense gratification is necessary in moderation. Moderation is unique for each person. Don't try to speculate your own path of moderation.

SIXTH LINE Do not allow a positive change in the situation to increase your false ego. The transition is not over yet. There are still many bumps on the road. You can pat yourself on the back when the transition is completed.

VISION

A world where everyone is united in Love for the Supreme Being despite caste and creed.

VALUES

Be compassionate towards animals. Animals are also spirit souls. See the opposite sex as mother or father. Be prepared to take responsibility for the consequences of union. Don't refuse your spouse.

For further information on the content of this book please contact:

Brian Burkea@gmail.com

TRIGRAMS

UPPER ▶ / LOWER ▼	CHEN Heaven	KHEN Storm	K'AN Liquid	KAN Solid	KUN Soil	SUN Wind	LI Fire	TUE Lake
CHEN Heaven	1	34	5	26	11	9	14	43
KHEN Storm	25	51	3	27	24	42	21	17
K'AN Liquid	6	40	29	4	7	59	64	47
KAN Solid	33	62	39	52	15	53	56	31
KUN Soil	12	16	8	23	2	20	35	45
SUN Wind	44	32	48	18	46	57	50	28
LI Fire	13	55	63	22	36	37	30	49
TUE Lake	10	54	60	41	19	61	38	58

CPSIA information can be obtained
at www.ICGtesting.com
Printed in the USA
LVHW080232090920
665411LV00019B/2004